zeno and the tortoise

zeno and the
tortoise

how to think like a philosopher

NICHOLAS FEARN

Atlantic Books
London

First published in Great Britain in 2001
by Atlantic Books, an imprint of Grove Atlantic Ltd

10 9 8 7 6 5 4 3 2 1

A CIP catalogue record for this book is available
from the British Library.

1 903809 13 4

Typeset by Palimpsest Book Production Limited, Polmont, Stirlingshire
Printed in Great Britain by CPD, Ebbw, Vale, Wales

Atlantic Books
An imprint of Grove Atlantic Ltd
29 Adam & Eve Mews
London W8 6UG

To Charlotte

Contents

Acknowledgements ix

Preface xi

1 Thales's Well 1

2 Protagoras and the Pigs 10

3 Zeno and the Tortoise 19

4 The Socratic Inquisition 25

5 Plato's Cave 31

6 Aristotle's Goals 41

7 Lucretius's Spear 50

8 Ockham's Razor 56

9 Machiavelli's Prince 61

10 Bacon's Chickens 67

11 Descartes' Demon 73

12 Hume's Fork 81

13 Reid's Common Sense 88

14 Rousseau's Contract 96

15 Kant's Spectacles 102

16 Bentham's Calculus 109

17 Hegel's Dialectic 116

18 Nietzsche's Hammer 122

Contents (continued)

19 The Young Wittgenstein's Mirror 130

20 The Older Wittgenstein's Games 137

21 Popper's Dolls 145

22 Ryle's University 150

23 Turing's Machine 158

24 Dawkins's Meme 165

25 Derrida and Deconstruction 173

Further Reading 181

Index 189

My chief thanks go to Herbert and Sheila Oakes, without whose help and encouragement over many years this book would not have been written.

I am also grateful to my publishers Toby Mundy and Alice Hunt, and to Julian Baggini, Jason Cowley, Tim Crane, Charlotte Foley, Daniel Ghossain, Tariq Goddard, Rebecca Ivatts and my former tutor Alan Thomas, whose teaching style sparked off the idea for this book.

Preface

There is a saying that goes, 'Don't learn the tricks of the trade, learn the trade', but some 'tricks' are very important to philosophers. Thinking rationally involves the deployment of the right philosophical tool at the right time, be it Ockham's Razor, Hume's Fork or some other device from the thinker's toolbox. The most enduring contributions of the great philosophers are the thinking tools, methods and approaches they invent or discover, which often outlive the theories and systems they construct or those that they use their tools to dismantle. This book attempts to take the reader from the earliest examples forged by the ancients through to some of the 'state of the art' equipment employed by today's professional philosophers. The object is to show not merely *what* the great philosophers thought, but to demonstrate *how* they thought. Some philosophers, such as William of Ockham and Gilbert Ryle, bequeathed ideas with very specific applications while others such as Thales and Nietzsche are included here for their general approaches and methods. What follows is not an exhaustive inventory, and many great thinkers are left out. Spinoza and Leibniz, for example, are omitted not because their innovations were unimportant or have not lasted, but out of a concern to present that information which is most useful and readily digestible to the general reader.

Being able to apply the techniques of philosophy is a great aid to understanding the doctrines of its greatest exponents. One need not be a violinist to appreciate Vivaldi, but the way in which we metabolize knowledge is different from the way we enjoy music. As thinking human beings, we tend not to feel confident with knowledge learned by rote. Knowing how to multiply by seven, for example, is not just a question of memorizing the seven times table. Children are told that two sevens are fourteen, that three sevens are twenty-one and so on, but do not understand multiplication until they can calculate beyond the examples already given, i.e. 13×7, 200×7 . . . Real understanding requires participation on the part of the learner. We only truly know something when we have applied it, manipulated it or added to it, and this book is designed to enable the reader to do likewise. Moreover, in illuminating how philosophers thought, I hope that non-specialist readers will find themselves able to think along similar lines. It is characteristic of those with genius that their work be wholly original, yet at the same time eminently duplicable. Methods that took philosophical mastery to devise do not necessarily require a philosophical master to reproduce them. Though works of philosophy are sometimes mysterious or impenetrable, the tools used to create them are often remarkably simple and can be quickly grasped and brought to bear on the reader's own thoughts.

Thales's Well
The world in a drop of water

In the summer of 1999, Cornell University published research purporting to show that love really is a drug. To be precise, it is a cocktail of dopamine, phenylethylamine and oxytocin in the bloodstream that produces the sensation we call infatuation. Love, the researchers argued, was in fact a chemically induced form of insanity. This condition lasts until the body builds up an immunity to the substances involved, which is usually just long enough to meet, mate and raise a child to early infancy. The theory sounds dubious, if not downright offensive. Love, we feel, is the most important thing that can happen to a person and should be placed on a pedestal, not in a syringe with which to inject the loveless. Cornell University's conclusions were based on the principle of 'reductionism': the thought that things can be understood by boiling them down to their component parts, or that complex, large-scale processes can be understood in terms of simpler ones. The research may be overturned sooner or later, but if it survives it will not be the first time our illusions have been dispelled by reductionist thinking.

Another example of reductionism is the belief that tonsillitis is caused by a certain kind of bacterium that has invaded the body, and that the best way to treat the illness is to tackle the germ directly by administering antibiotics. An alternative tactic – though not one advised by many Western doctors – would be to regard the illness as a malady of the whole body, caused, perhaps, by an 'imbalance' in the individual's entire system. Such a 'holistic' approach will suggest various treatments that may or may not be effective. In very general cases of poor health, a holistic view of the situation may be the most sensible one, or at least an important accompaniment to the reductive approach. Mild heart conditions, for instance, are sometimes treated not with drugs, but by the patient giving up smoking, cutting down their cholesterol intake and taking regular exercise. Even this advice, however, is the product of reductionist investigations into body chemistry and physiology.

Despite the scientific advances it has given us, reductionism is something of a dirty word today. Some of us think that in attempting to understand the universe, we sully it. What it took God divine grace to create, we inspect through intrusive microscopes and disseminate in barbarous human tongues. Armed with the new genetic sciences, a botanist can claim to have decoded the essence of a rose in the plant's genome. He or she would be given short shrift by poets such as William Blake, who famously complained that science 'murders to dissect', or the nineteenth-century aesthete Walter Pater, who wrote that a scientist's garden would have 'written labels fluttering on the stalks for blooms'. Even if we do not all recoil so violently from reductionism, many of us feel instinctively that it must deal in crude simplifications, or works to 'bring nature down to our level'. But our level is the only one we have, and there need not be anything wrong with it. The American physicist Richard Feynman argued that we should not be unduly modest about our faculties, remarking that, as a scientist, he could not only appreciate the aesthetic beauty of a flower, but also marvel at its intricate biochemical structures. At the same time, however, we have suffered the follies of Freud and Marx, who reduced too much of human experience to sex and economics respectively. Reduction is a tool that can be misused, but we must remember that it gave us space travel and the Human Genome Project.

The first reductionist philosopher – and also the first Western philosopher of any description – was Thales, a Greek born around 636 BC at Miletus in Asia Minor (now Turkey).

Thales was one of the Seven Sages, the men of the sixth and seventh centuries BC who were renowned for their wisdom as rulers, lawgivers and counsellors. Their maxims were inscribed on the walls of the temple of Apollo at Delphi. Across the ancient world, mosaics were reproduced depicting their aged, bearded heads alongside such phrases as 'Know thyself' and 'Nothing in excess'. Thales travelled as far as Egypt and Babylonia to gather knowledge from other cultures. When he returned home and offered his own contribution to knowledge, the Greeks hailed him as the founder of science, mathematics and philosophy. Part of his fame stemmed from a legend told one hundred and fifty years later by the historian Herodotus. Using the astronomy he had learned in the East (or, according to other authorities, by making a lucky guess), Thales successfully predicted that there would be an eclipse of the sun in 585 BC. On that day, the armies of Mede and Lydia were marching into battle against one another. They interpreted the eclipse as a warning from the gods and quickly broke off hostilities to sign a peace treaty. Modern astronomers have shown that the eclipse must have occurred on 28 May. This means that the aborted battle is the only event in the ancient world that we can date precisely.

Plato (428–347 BC) tells the story of how Thales was walking along studying the stars one evening when he fell down a well. A pretty servant girl heard the philosopher's cries and helped him out of the well, but not without quipping that Thales was a man 'who studies the stars yet cannot even see the ground at his feet'. This seems unfair, as Thales's head was not always in the clouds. There are several tales attesting to his practical skills. He urged a political union of the Greek city-states of Ionia as the only way to hold back the expansionist aims of their rival, Lydia. Though the authorities ignored him, his advice proved to be apposite over the centuries that followed. Aristotle (384–322 BC) relates that Thales was reproached for his poverty, which was taken to prove that philosophy is of no use to anyone. In response, Thales used his skills to predict that the following season's olive crop would be a bumper harvest. He then bought up all the olive presses in Miletus (presumably by taking out a loan) and made a fortune when the yield matched his expectations. Thales died at the age of seventy-eight of heat exhaustion while watching an athletics match. The inscription on his tomb read: 'Here in a narrow tomb great Thales lies; yet his renown for wisdom reached the skies.'

There is no evidence that Thales wrote any books, but he apparently said that he would be satisfied if those who passed on his ideas attributed them to him rather than to themselves. Given his belief that the universe was made out of water, most of us would be more than pleased to oblige. Water, Thales argued, was the fundamental substance of which all others were composed. Matter was condensed water and air was evaporated water. The entire earth, he maintained, was a disc floating on a giant lake, the waves and ripples of which caused earthquakes. According to Aristotle, Thales's first inkling of this came from observing that water was essential to all forms of life in the natural world. Thales's theory seems a reasonable stab at the truth when we consider that water comes in solid, liquid and vaporous forms. Though mistaken, the idea was the first scientific hypothesis ever recorded.

Thales was making a grand reduction. The properties of all the objects in the world, be they metals, mountains, gases or people, were reducible to just one set of properties – those of water. So if you ground things finely enough, dissected them thinly enough or examined them closely enough, you would not find iron or stone or flesh, but water. It might seem strange that anyone would want to explain one thing in terms of another rather than treating it on its own terms, but this is how reduction proceeds. If we desire to understand the world, then this means putting things in terms we can understand. Reducing something is like translating it into a more intelligible language. After reduction, a phenomenon is easier to handle and less mysterious because components are simpler to comprehend than a whole system.

However, if simplification were the only aim, many of our modern-day reductions would be failures. As far as we know, Thales did not go into great detail as to exactly how water forms the various phenomena of the natural world, but at least water is a substance with which we are all well acquainted. The mathematics of modern atomic theory, on the other hand, is comprehensible only to a small group of people with the proper training. While reduction renders things more intelligible, this does not necessarily mean more intelligible to everyone. Since the common understanding of the many is so frequently replaced by the better understanding of the few, reductionism is bound to arouse a measure of distrust. This is compounded by the fact that, in terms of explanations, simpler often means more brutely physical, so that to be a reductionist is often to be a materialist. Reductionists are also hampered by an unfortunate choice of terms. All that reduction truly 'reduces' is the complexity of an explanation. Everything else to be explained about the phenomenon is preserved. However, this is only as long as there is a real phenomenon to reduce. Reductionists are more than happy to jettison such things as souls and gods which they might not believe in. Though simpler explanations are deemed 'lower' because they are closer to the most basic facts we know, we could equally well call them 'higher' because they rise above irrelevant and obfuscating details to cut to the essential truth of things. The hierarchy of knowledge and understanding that reductionism yields could then be viewed as an ordinary pyramid rather than an inverted one.

Since reduction is about simplification, there is always the risk of oversimplification. It pays, therefore, to be careful about what exactly is being reduced and just what explanatory powers the reduction has. The question has to be asked whether in reducing something we have merely eliminated it from our description of the world. The taste of apricots, for example, could be reduced to the interplay of the molecules of the fruit with the receptors in our palate. But does this not ignore the sensation of what apricots actually taste like? After all, someone could know about the chemical constituents of apricots without ever having eaten one. Even so, elimination might not be all bad. Human understanding progresses by two means: gathering facts to discover new phenomena, and drawing these phenomena together under the simplifying influence of reductive explanations. Sometimes we find that as soon as the available evidence has been adequately reduced, new data appears that casts that reduction into doubt and demands that we look at the whole of the phenomenon once again.

It is paradoxical that in order to understand familiar natural processes, such as why water evaporates when boiled, we need to consult 'lower' levels of organization and unfamiliar entities such as protons and electrons. It would be strange to suggest that the 'higher' levels of organization we are used to dealing with – that of clouds, cups of coffee and human tears – are in fact illusory. Scientific reductionists sometimes come perilously close to asserting this when they say that we are 'nothing but mounds of atoms'. The key words here are 'nothing but'. This is correct if we mean it in the same sense that a novel is 'nothing but' a collection of ink marks on paper or a brain is 'nothing but' an agglomeration of neurones. If humans are simply mounds of atoms, then this says less about the dusty origin of humanity than it does about the amazing potential of otherwise harmless-looking atoms.

However, there is another way in which a reductionist might claim that only the most basic levels of description denote what is truly real. Nature seems to make most of her big decisions on the microscopic level. As the American philosopher Jerry Fodor (1935–) remarked, there is no science of Tuesdays. Science recognizes only four forces: gravity, electromagnetism and the strong and weak nuclear forces that hold atomic nuclei together. The weak nuclear force has been shown to be a form of the electromagnetic force, and it is hoped that before long all the forces will be discovered to be aspects of a single unifying force. According to hard-core scientific reductionists, everything that happens is because of these forces and nothing else (especially not ethereal concepts like human intentions). They operate upon macroscopic objects such as cars because they work upon the atoms of which these are composed. To explain every natural process in terms of the operation of the four forces is to suggest that the only adequate explanations are those that refer to microscopic events. We might, for instance, say that a spell of hot weather caused a drought which caused the crops to fail. A truly accurate explanation, however, would speak of the increased agitation of air molecules rather than in mere metaphors such as 'heat'. If someone asks me how I got to the party and I say that I drove there, I would not expect to be corrected on the grounds that, in actual fact, I depressed a pedal and refined petroleum combusted to generate propulsion. I would be even more confused if my interrogator immediately began talking about chemical reactions and carbon compounds. The more drastic the reduction, the greater the need to show how it ties in with our ordinary concepts – otherwise we may not believe that the reductionist is talking about the same things as the rest of us. Something in our ordinary experience, be it the action of driving to the party or the taste of apricots in the canapés, must be preserved in a reduction for it to count as an explanation *of* something. Otherwise we have merely listened to a stand-alone speech on an irrelevant topic rather than an answer to a question about my means of transport. On the other hand, the reductionist's explanation may be more welcome if I had suffered a breakdown on the way because I had filled my car with the wrong kind of petrol.

The four forces of nature may underpin everything from the movement of the clouds to the recipe for lasagne, but a physicist's understanding of those forces would not itself enable one to predict the weather like a meteorologist or make pasta like a top Italian chef. (Perhaps in the future there will exist robot chefs with a complete knowledge of the fundamental forces along with a superhuman ability to utilize that knowledge. It might be possible for such a creature to concoct the perfect dish through brute force of number-crunching, but this would seem an unnecessarily long-winded way to go about one of life's simple pleasures.) On the other hand, being able to cook well or give an accurate weather forecast are skills far removed from an ultimate understanding of the universe. For that task, reductionist thinking is clearly required. This does not mean that reductionism is *only* useful to explain the subatomic physics of life. You can usually understand something better by reducing it and looking at the level of explanation immediately below it. For example, you can cook a better lasagne if you understand the correct measures of flour and tomato sauce in its recipe. To understand flour, you would need in turn to understand the level below that – that is, the consistency of the various grains used in the production of flour, so that you only choose the finest durum wheat for your ingredients. One could go on down the levels of explanation until atoms and molecules are reached. By the time you have decided on the best quantity of hydrogen to use, however, you will most likely have died of starvation. Usually, it is the level immediately below a phenomenon that is most helpful in comprehending it rather than ever more basic and abstruse levels of description. The great thing about reductive explanations is that they allow you to work upwards again, like a ship's captain taking a trip to the engine room and returning to the bridge better informed about the capabilities of his vessel. You descend to more basic levels of description to zero in on what will make all the difference on higher levels.

Despite the practical uses of reductionism, its application in everyday life often comes in the form of cynicism. It is reductionist to say, for example, that though someone gives money to charity and devotes his free time to volunteer work, he is 'merely' serving his own interests. It is also reductionist to declare that although a company might instigate projects aimed at improving the environment and protecting its employees, it is ultimately concerned 'only' for its long-term profits. That said, it would be no less reductionist to claim that the company is acting solely out of Christian kindness. To qualify as reductionist, an explanation needs only to explain one thing in terms of another that is more basic, or many things in terms of a single other thing. Reductionism sounds quite innocent when put like this, but nothing that has so much explanatory power is ever going to be harmless.

2 | Protagoras and the Pigs
Is man the measure of all things?

The pop star Sting, in his efforts to save the rain forests, campaigned in the 1980s for the rights of the Kayapo Indians of the Amazon to preserve their way of life. He successfully petitioned the president of Brazil to establish an Indian reserve, and in 1991 the tribe was granted a protected area of around 25,000 square miles. No sooner had the agreement been concluded, however, than the Kayapo chiefs began to cut deals with mining and logging companies. This made them multi-million-dollar fortunes which they reportedly spent on houses, cars and planes while providing little for their villagers. Despite illustrating credulousness on the one hand and cynicism on the other, this cautionary tale has a positive moral. It shows that human beings strive for much the same things even though we are divided by cultural chasms. A shared fondness for fast food and automobiles has been easier to achieve than globalization of human rights, but it is a start at least. Some moralists suggest that the reason we have not yet attained this panacea is because there are no universal values that apply to everyone in all cultures. Instead, they argue, one way of doing things is as valid as any other, and acts are right or wrong only with reference to a particular cultural system. This is the doctrine of relativism. Today's relativists have gone even further and claim that each individual creates his or her own system of values. The view that 'everything is a matter of opinion' is commonplace. Everyone is entitled to their own beliefs, it is asserted, and no one's perspective is more or less right than anyone else's.

The father of relativism was Protagoras. Born in Thrace in around 485 BC, Protagoras was the first of the ancient Greek sophists, the travelling rhetoricians who taught wisdom for money. The particular brand of wisdom they espoused was the kind that earned Greek gentlemen their points on the debating floor and in the law courts. A good sophist was able to win an argument even if he was in the wrong. The Sicilian rhetorician Gorgias (483–378 BC) maintained, moreover, that knowledge of the subject under debate was unnecessary because every position was false and words have no fixed meaning beyond their use to cajole and persuade. For this reason, the sophists are not thought of as philosophers in the true sense of the word. They should not be dismissed as scoundrels, however, as their ethos was based on a distrust of so-called objective Truth. This was itself a philosophical position, and one that has had to wait until the present day for its renaissance.

Protagoras was arguably the most celebrated sophist of all and amassed a great fortune from the high fees he commanded during his forty-year career. He boasted genuine skill in poetry, grammar and jurisprudence and personally drafted the constitution for the Greek colony of Thurii in southern Italy. He was fêted by the Athenians on his first visit to their city, but was exiled in 415 BC for writing the first ever agnostic tract. 'With regard to the gods,' he began, 'I cannot feel sure either that they are or that they are not, nor what they are like in figure; for there are many things that hinder sure knowledge, the obscurity of the knowledge and the shortness of human life.' Protagoras died five years later, just before his seventieth birthday when the ship taking him to Sicily was lost at sea. His books were publicly burned, and only a few fragments of his works survive. We know about his ideas chiefly through the writings of other thinkers, including Plato in whose dialogues he appears, though only in order to be demolished by Socrates.

Protagoras's most famous doctrine was that 'Man is the measure of all things', meaning that there is no truth except that which man perceives. The basis of this view is that nothing in the world can sustain its nature by itself. Instead, things acquire their nature by their interaction with other things. Nothing just *is* but rather everything is in a process of coming to be, and this coming to be is becoming relative to something else. The colour white, for example, is neither inside nor outside your eyes. Rather, it is the result of an interaction between yourself and something that you perceive. This is held to be the case for all perceptual qualities. If the wind feels hot to me and cold to you, then it is both hot-to-me and cold-to-you. This does not mean that the wind is both hot and cold, as it does not possess a temperature in itself but only in its relationships with those who feel it. The way something is perceived by a given person is a matter for the object and its perceiver and no one else. The fact that another individual finds the wind cold does not mean that it does not feel warm to me. Since things only acquire their specific nature in the way that they are perceived by someone, I can never be said to be wrong in the way that I perceive something. I cannot be contradicted by the nature of the object, as it has no nature without my perception, and I cannot be contradicted by someone else's testimony, since their perceptions have no bearing on my own.

There is an immediate problem here because some people are clearly insane. Someone may think he is Napoleon, but that does not make him the conqueror of the Iberian peninsula. On Protagoras's account, this individual really could be Napoleon *to himself*, for 'Napoleon' and his psychiatrist are perceiving two different things rather than disagreeing about the same thing. This is because the nature of a thing is determined by an interaction between the object and the perceiver, and I am a different perceiver when I am insane than when I am healthy in mind. Protagoras therefore concludes that none of his perceptions can ever be mistaken and that all false belief is in fact impossible.

At this point in Plato's dialogue *Theaetetus*, Socrates asks Protagoras why he should stop at the judgements of all human beings being equal. Isn't this unfair on pigs, for example? Why shouldn't the judgements of swine be as valid as those of humans? Protagoras chose to bite this bullet, though he soon spat it out again. He replied that pigs are perfectly entitled to their own opinions, in so far as they can have them. Unfortunately, this would mean that Protagoras's pupils were paying good money to be taught opinions which were no wiser than those of a pig. Yet Protagoras claimed to be an expert on virtue and to teach special knowledge. Since everyone's perceptions are equally true, the sophist argued, wisdom must be something other than making true judgements. Certain opinions are wiser and better to hold than others, he said, not because they are more true, but because they are more beneficial to the lives of those who hold them. Some beliefs will make you more successful in law and politics, for example, and these are the ones that Protagoras imparted for a fee.

Even a teacher as wise as Protagoras, however, might make mistakes or lead someone astray. An apocryphal story tells of how he once gave instruction to a young man on the basis that he would waive his fee should the pupil fail to win his first case in the law courts. The pupil's first case was one brought by Protagoras himself to ensure the recovery of his fee. Perhaps the young man had tried to catch his teacher in a double bind – either he wins the case and does not have to pay, or he loses and Protagoras cannot claim recompense if he is to be true to his word. Assuming that the latter broke his promise, his pupil would not have found the lessons Protagoras had taught him to have been very beneficial. He would more likely curse his gullibility in mistakenly believing that his teacher's instruction would help him win public favour and professional success in court. Nor would he find it any consolation that his confidence in Protagoras had been true *for him* at the time. In fact, he was mistaken precisely because the truth of his belief was not a relative one dependent upon his perceptions – which had missed entirely his instructor's preference for collecting his fees over keeping his promises. One does not have to besmirch the reputation of Protagoras further to find parallel examples. People often make mistakes about what is good for them. When we are unwell, a doctor's judgement about what will make us better is usually more reliable than our own. This is because a doctor's diagnosis is more likely to be true than our own, and not just true *for the doctor* but true *per se*.

If Protagoras had not had a vested interest in defending his qualifications as a teacher, he might have retained without caveat the view that none of us are any wiser than pigs, or at least that no one is wiser than anyone else. There are, after all, many people around today who dismiss the advice of dead, white European males as the biased product of a narrow political agenda. Others prefer alternative forms of treatment to those prescribed in conventional Western medicine. More generous individuals accept at the same time that qualified physicians and DWEMs are also entitled to their own views. The idea is that truth is a matter of taste like anything else, and that it is the individual's right to choose his or her own way of seeing things rather than have someone else's views imposed upon them. There is one way of seeing things in particular, however, that does not fit into this account of truth: namely, the view that relativism is incorrect. If everyone is entitled to their own opinion, what can the relativist say of someone else's opinion that truth is not relative? If this alternative view is to be valid along with all others, then it is equally true that relativism is false.

The case for relativism cannot be stated without paradox. Either relativism must be as false as it is true, or a special case must be made for the truth of relativism. But if it is to be an objective fact that truth is relative, and not a mere opinion, then how is it that truth cannot be more than a matter of taste in other spheres too? The belief that different moral systems can lead to equally stable and happy societies rests on the experiences of travellers and anthropologists. By accepting their findings we endorse the method of observation that led to them. This method, however, is transferable to other disciplines and areas where it might not yield relativistic conclusions. Economists who visited both East and West Germany in the 1980s could easily judge from what they saw around them that a planned economy is not as effective at creating wealth as the free market. Relativism is refuted every time a truth in any area is allowed to be non-relative, and this includes the area of relativism itself. The relativist wants to have his cake and eat it, but one cannot without self-contradiction assert that relativism is objectively true and that truth is not objective. It is fortunate that this is the case, for there are worse things to believe than that you are Napoleon. We would not want to say that someone like Adolf Hitler was entitled to his opinions, or that his were no less true than anyone else's.

The wider conclusions of Protagoras may be self-refuting, but he did hit upon an important insight. This is the thought that every truth requires a measure of some kind. Truths are not true of and in themselves, but are true within a system of thought, or according to certain rules that test their veracity. This would be the case even if there were only one objective measure of truth. It is unequivocally true that two plus two equals four, but only because four is always the result when we apply the rules of addition correctly. The value of a pair of shoes, on the other hand, may be different according to whether they are given to a beggar or a king, but in each case their value is a value *to* someone. In both cases, the measure of the truth is external to what it evaluates. How we are to evaluate the measure is another issue, and one that does not always have an easy answer. It will certainly not do to say that this measure is simply 'reality' or 'the way things are', since how we divine the nature of things is precisely what is in question.

The problem is especially important in the realm of moral values. People's beliefs about what is right and wrong vary according to the culture in which they live or were brought up. In the Irish Republic, abortion is regarded as a sin even when the mother's life is at risk, whereas in China abortion is regarded as a moral duty performed for the greater good of population control. It is tempting to conclude that the moral buck stops with the particular society we live in. That very thought leads many to preach unconditional tolerance of other cultures. However, the fact that there are many different moral systems does not justify this position, for tolerance is just another social value that may or may not be correct within a given culture. To suggest that it has a purchase beyond that is to admit that there are higher laws above those of the world's individual cultures. There is also a self-refuting element in the argument, since we do not tolerate cultures such as Nazism. Yet Nazism was a fully-fledged moral system with its own standards of right and wrong, its own practices and its own nascent traditions, albeit a system in which racial hatred was a virtue. Cultural tolerance as we understand it in the West may be a very fine thing, but it is logically hollow if we only tolerate the cultures that do not deviate too far from our own. Worse, we sometimes refuse to see certain aspects of other cultures that depart from our own and are tolerant where perhaps we should not be. Many visitors to Soviet Russia and Mao's China accepted that the Russians and Chinese had 'their own way of doing things' at the time, even though that way involved repression and mass murder. And it is not only military dictatorships that deny people their basic human rights, but also many forest-dwelling tribes and religious denominations. Be that as it may, after observing the multifarious cultures of the world most of us cannot help but feel that we should be tolerant towards them and refrain from the worst excesses of patriotic chauvinism. Even if we believe that there is a single correct way of doing things (or at least one that is the best) we might be less than certain that our own culture is the one that has got it right.

At the same time, to argue that all cultures are equally valid is to deny the notion of any kind of moral progress. Five hundred years ago, Europeans were burning each other at the stake in the name of morality. We do not hesitate to condemn such behaviour as wicked. Should we react any differently if people of another culture on the other side of the world were to revive the practice today? What would allow us to condemn them is a notion of what is good for all individual human beings as thinking, feeling creatures. While there is great cultural diversity across the world, it should not be forgotten that there is much that all cultures hold in common. For example, it is difficult to find a culture in which the random killing of children is regarded as a good thing. So rare is this practice that, should we find a people for whom arbitrary infanticide is a cherished institution, we would do better to investigate the practice properly rather than jump to the conclusion that they hold child killing to be virtuous in itself. They may believe, for instance, that the gods demand child sacrifice if they are to make the crops grow. On further investigation, we may find that these people desire the same things that the rest of us do, such as health, wealth and happiness, and merely have odd (or tragically mistaken) ways of going about acquiring them.

Common ground is evident whenever two cultures meet and morality is discussed. If two different cultures had nothing in common in their morality, a moral dialogue could never begin between them. No culture is an island, and to date it has always been possible to establish diplomatic moral relations with newly discovered societies. Even a relationship of mutual hatred provides common ground, for this at least shows that the opponents are considering the same kind of thing in their dispute. Similarly, if there were no degrees of temperature that we could agree upon, where we could both opine that the wind or the water was hot or cold, we would never be able to disagree. It is because we understand and agree upon the terms 'hot' and 'cold' that we can have an argument when we wish to apply them differently in a given case. Disagreements require agreement somewhere along the line.

There may, of course, be tribes of rain-forest Indians who, after receiving the support of a pop star and having seen what other cultures have to offer, would prefer to remain in the state of nature and continue to live on nuts and caterpillars, cheerfully suffering the depredations of malaria and prolonged exposure to the elements. If they are willing to endure this condition in order to maintain their traditions then that is their choice, although we should also ask whether it is the choice of the people or merely of their leaders (who may have the most to lose if the basic structures of society change). If it is what the people want, and what successive generations want, then perhaps they have a moral code that is fundamentally incommensurable with our own. This conclusion would be even stronger if their traditions included infanticide, incest and habitual murder. There may be social systems in which these practices represent the height of virtue, but anthropologists have never discovered them. Should they ever be discovered, and their practices revealed not to reflect mistaken beliefs about gods or crops, then it would be more intelligible to assume not that that was their morality, but that this people did not have morality as a part of their culture.

Protagoras might have agreed with this point. He thought that no individual's beliefs could be reconciled with those of another because they were about quite different things in every case. What he did not realize was that such a state of affairs would prohibit us from ever communicating, for communication requires common ground. Though we may not know what the true, objective measure of things should be, we will not discover it by dismissing the views of others as true only *for them*. No matter how much respect this attitude shows for the beliefs of other people, it demonstrates little for their capabilities as thinking beings.

3 | Zeno and the Tortoise
The use of *reductio ad absurdum*

There is a common suspicion in the more refined bar rooms that homophobia, far from denoting red-blooded heterosexuality, in fact belies an inability to cope with one's own repressed homosexual leanings. But if hatred of others springs from hatred of oneself, then by the same token we would expect Ku Klux Klan members, for example, to have a repressed African-American side to their personality. This line of ridicule is known as *reductio ad absurdum*, which means literally 'reduce to absurdity'. We use this device whenever, instead of arguing that a position is untrue, we examine what would follow if it were correct in order to derive unacceptable results. In ordinary life, ridiculing someone else's argument is certainly easier than constructing a position of one's own. It is no different in philosophy. Where we must wait for the passage of time to reveal the absurdity of a government policy or an over-hasty marriage, in logical argument the process is altogether quicker.

The first philosopher to employ *reductio ad absurdum* was Zeno, who (according to Plato) was a tall and graceful Greek born around 490 BC in Elea, a town now in southern Italy. Zeno was a pupil of the philosopher Parmenides, who taught that all the many and varied things that seem to exist are actually a single everlasting reality that he called 'being'. He argued that the negation of being, along with any imagined changes it might undergo, is in fact impossible. Only about two hundred words of Zeno's writings survive, but it seems that as a young man he wrote a work of philosophy with which he may not have been entirely pleased and which was circulated without his knowledge. The book did, however, make him famous in faraway Athens. Plato relates that Parmenides and Zeno visited the city together in around 450 BC where they met the young Socrates. Zeno stayed a while, charging noblemen for the privilege of listening to him hold forth. According to legend, he became involved in politics on his return to Elea and plotted to overthrow the city's tyrant, Nearchus. Before the conspirators could act, Zeno was arrested and tortured to death for his treason. Several stories tell of his interrogation. In one, he named the tyrant's friends as his co-conspirators rather than betraying his accomplices. In others, he bit off his tongue and spat it at Nearchus or even leaped upon the tyrant and bit off his nose. These tales are not as far-fetched as Zeno's own philosophy.

Zeno wanted to prove that the multiplicity that the world exhibits was an illusion and that reality was composed of an eternally unchanging oneness. He disavowed any notion of time, motion or any kind of plurality among objects. He attacked our ordinary notions of space and time by assuming their truth and taking the consequences as far as they would go. The result of Zeno's efforts was a collection of forty paradoxes. Most of these have been lost, but three of them in particular have been causing problems for philosophers and mathematicians for two and a half millennia.

The most famous of Zeno's paradoxes is the story of a race between Achilles and the tortoise. Since Achilles is a very fast runner, the tortoise is given a ten-yard head-start. This may not sound terribly generous to the tortoise, but in fact it is enough to win him the contest. When the race begins, Achilles is quick off the mark and soon makes up those ten yards. By this time the tortoise has managed to advance just one yard, which Achilles then covers in a single bound. Now, however, the tortoise has managed to advance a further three inches. Picking up speed, Achilles crosses those inches only to find that the tortoise has moved on an extra inch. By the time Achilles traverses that inch, the tortoise will in turn have advanced some further distance, albeit a very short one. Zeno argues that no matter how fast Achilles runs he will never be able to overtake his rival, because in order to do so he must first draw level with him. This can never be achieved because as long as it takes Achilles some time – however little – to reach the tortoise's position, the creature will have had time to move on a fraction. Though the distance separating them draws ever shorter, it can never dwindle to nothing. The tortoise will therefore remain in the lead for ever.

If this is not frustrating enough for Achilles, things get even worse for him in the paradox of the racetrack. In order to reach the end of a course, Achilles would first have to reach the halfway mark. After that, the remaining distance would have its own halfway mark to be reached. The final quarter can also be divided into two, and so on, it seems, for ever. To get to the finishing line, Achilles would have to travel through an infinite number of divisions of the track. Since each one of these segments must comprise some distance and take some time, however minute, to cross, it will take him for ever to finish the course. Each segment may be very small, but an infinite number of them will make for an infinite distance. Fortunately, or unfortunately, Achilles will not have to worry about running until the end of time as, by the same reasoning, he will never be able to begin running. The first half of the track can also be divided ad infinitum, so before Achilles can cover half the distance he must first cover a quarter of it, and before that an eighth and so on . . . Since there is no end to these fractions, it will take him literally for ever to leave the starting blocks.

According to the paradox of the arrow, these problems can be put aside because nothing ever moves. The flight of an arrow can be divided into instants, which are the smallest possible measure of time. If the arrow moves during one of these instants, it means that it begins the instant in one place and ends in another. In this case we would not be talking about an instant at all because the moment could be divided further.

Once we have alighted on a true instant – a moment that by definition cannot be divided further – then we have a division of time in which no movement can take place. This, however, means that the arrow can never move, as no amount of no-motion can add up to motion. Since the arrow does not move in any single point in its flight, it does not move over the whole flight.

The arrow is the easiest of the paradoxes to tackle. Motion requires time, so it is not surprising that if you take away time and talk instead of instants then you also take away motion. Though the arrow may not move in any given instant, it can still move if motion is defined as a thing's appearance in a different place at a later point in time. The paradoxes involving Achilles and the tortoise are more difficult. They can still be avoided, Zeno argued, by dismissing the very notion of divisibility. If this offends common sense, he thought, then too bad for common sense. It is clearly unsatisfactory, however, to replace one absurdity with another as Zeno does. Fortunately, we can escape from the predicament by using mathematical tools that were not available to the philosopher and his contemporaries in the fifth century BC. We now know it to be a mistake to suppose that a distance composed of an infinite number of finite parts must itself be infinite. If we were to construct a series which added $\frac{1}{2}$ to $\frac{1}{4}$ to $\frac{1}{8}$ and so on for ever, most mathematicians would avow that the total is one, not infinity. There is therefore nothing impossible in space being infinitely divisible. Neither is there a problem with crossing an infinite number of segments of a racecourse in a finite time. By this thinking, then, Achilles can leave his starting blocks and overtake the tortoise unhindered before being shot in the heel with a well-aimed arrow.

Zeno was a 'strong' user of *reductio* because he took a set of beliefs and derived logical impossibilities from them. But one does not have to come up with paradoxes to stay true to the method. 'Weaker' reductios may involve consequences that are merely unacceptable rather than impossible. A pro-life philosopher, for example, might reject any moral system the tenets of which imply support for abortion even if such support is not explicitly articulated. Or a political theorist might dismiss revolutionary communism because it can countenance the death of innocents as a justifiable means to an end even though its adherents do not hold the right to murder as a core principle. On this level, *reductio ad absurdum* is little more than an arguing technique, as one man's absurdity might not seem so ridiculous to another. The point goes beyond matters of moral taste – such as abortion – into the purely logical. The German philosopher Immanuel Kant (1724–1804) argued that theft was wrong because such behaviour could not be universalized. That is, if everyone went around stealing things it would undermine the convention of property that makes theft possible in the first place. This *reductio* would not convince everyone, but it would convince a thief least of all. A similar argument was presented to Yossarian, the hero of Joseph Heller's *Catch-22*, when he refused to fly in any more bombing raids. 'What would happen,' his commanding officer asked, 'if everyone refused to fly?' 'Then I'd be a damn fool to do any different,' Yossarian replied. The efficacy of *reductio ad absurdum* depends in a large part upon shared notions of the ridiculous.

An equally important issue for all kinds of *reductio* is whether absurdities that arise in extreme situations should be allowed to impinge upon beliefs that hold true in ordinary circumstances. For example, many people believe that there is no harm in the occasional use of marijuana and that the law against the drug infringes their liberty. The anti-drugs lobby routinely counters that if the law allowed people to do anything they wanted, society would break down. This may well be true, but it is a consequence far removed from smoking the occasional joint. The charge that someone is taking a point to extremes is normally sufficient to blunt the force of a *reductio* in ordinary life. For the most part, the further a *reductio* is taken towards the extreme, the less we feel bound to take notice of its upshot. This may be due to cynicism rather than credulity, since there might be no position that cannot be reduced to some form of absurdity or another.

The other defence against *reductio* is to claim that one's beliefs are not philosophical ones. That is, they are about specific concerns rather than lofty generalities. So an explanation of homophobia does not have to explain every other kind of hatred. What is true of homophobes may not be true of race-baiting rednecks, though it is possible the two might sometimes be one and the same. However, to defend an explanation is also to defend the method used to construct it. In our original case, this is the dubious principle that all hatred is really self-hatred. Ultimately, for *reductio* to work it is necessary for both sides to agree on what conclusions count as 'unacceptable'. For that reason, the approach may be unlikely ever to convince the proponents of soft-drug legalization.

4 | The Socratic Inquisition
Uncovering truth by interrogation

To the delight of politicians and the chagrin of philosophers, many people can be convinced of just about anything so long as one does not employ rational argument. Ancient Greek sophists such as Protagoras and Gorgias, however, were dealing with a more receptive audience. There were few entertainments more appealing to noblemen living in the fifth century BC than listening to the debates of great speakers. As participants in the democratic system of the day, a grounding in the art of rhetoric at the feet of a professional sophist was an essential part of young aristocrats' education. If today's political classes have rejected the virtues of a classical education, they make a much lamented exception in the case of the sophist's art. At the time of writing, Britain's governing Labour Party sends its would-be spin doctors on special training weekends where they learn how to avoid answering a straight question. One advanced exercise involves a face-to-face examination in which the candidate is asked simply, 'What is the time?' If the subject can hold out for fifteen minutes without giving the answer, they are through to the next stage. What the next stage consists of no one has yet revealed, and if they ever do it would probably not be wise to believe them. Such dissemblers practised their skill unmolested until the arrival of Socrates (469–399 BC), who discovered, or rediscovered, something that was kryptonite to sophists: the truth. Socrates administered this poison through the device now known as the Socratic method, a relentless battery of questions designed to undermine a position using the sophist's own words and admissions.

Socrates possessed the perfect constitution for a battle of

wills. He was a man who would meditate barefoot in the snow for days or, on the point of entering a friend's house, pause for hours on the threshold while he scrutinized a philosophical problem in silence. A robust individual, he distinguished himself as a soldier in his early life and boasted a prodigious capacity for alcohol. He died at the age of seventy, leaving two small children – one apparently an infant in arms. Socrates was also famously ugly. A traveller skilled in reading faces once told him he had the face of a monster who was capable of any crime, to which the philosopher replied, 'You know me, sir!' Others were more charitable. The young blade Alcibiades likened Socrates to a statue of the hideous Silenus that opens to show beauties hidden within. Alcibiades apparently considered this remark to constitute flirting, which only goes to show that the Greeks were considerably thicker-skinned than ourselves.

If allowances were made for his appearance, Socrates exploited them to good effect. As an old man, he asked his opponents to consider his age and keep their answers brief and to the point so that he would not lose the thread. He was not worried about his own concentration, but that of the assembled spectators. If men were to gain the full benefit of his thought, they would need to learn how to listen. They would need to pay close attention to the content of questions and answers rather than simply marvelling at their aesthetic merit. Phrasing one's assertions as questions is a recognized debating tactic for today's sophists, but Socrates is not regarded as the founder of Western philosophy because of his rhetorical skills. The aim of Socratic method is not merely to win the argument but to discover the absolute truth of the matter. One must always strive for the truth, Socrates held, even if that involves standing corrected and losing a debate. Socrates was not in the habit of losing debates, but there were times when he acknowledged a stalemate. While this involved admitting his ignorance at the end of a debate as strongly as he professed it at the outset, it was never without the proviso that his opponent was equally afflicted.

For someone who eventually overturned an establishment single-handedly, Socrates was curiously modest. Unlike the sophists, he charged no fees and even declared himself incompetent to teach. Whereas modern-day inquisitors might decline to give their personal opinions while roasting those of others, Socrates was quite candid in declaring his own position – which he claimed was one of ignorance. It was for this cheerful admission that the Delphic Oracle famously pronounced him the wisest man in Greece. If, as he claimed, the only thing he knew was that he knew nothing, this did not prevent him from expounding his own opinions at length. His modesty is often irony, while his praise for the wisdom of others is usually sarcasm. There is a deeper sense, however, in which his modesty does betray integrity. Having urged that we must 'follow the argument where it leads', it makes good sense also to resolve that one will not hold dogmatically to any beliefs with which one began the argument. This means being ready to take criticism as well as to back propositions. It is possible to treat even politicians unfairly, after all.

Socrates certainly had an agenda and he espoused a complex philosophical system. But he did not believe the truth to be something that belonged to him as such – like an original thesis which was his to impart at will. Rather, the truth was something immanent in the world and in men, which he could draw out through reasoned questioning. So, rather than promote himself (like the sophists) as a great repository of wisdom, Socrates likened himself to a midwife who delivers the truth. In practice, he routinely asked recognized experts to offer their definition of a concept such as justice, courage or the good. The early stages of an argument were then constructed in ponderous detail one step at a time, with the philosopher making apparently innocuous remarks and his interlocutor intoning the mantra: 'Yes, that is so, Socrates.' Socrates would then increase the content of his questions until he found a belief held by his opponent that was both true and at odds with the latter's initial position. Further questioning followed until an acceptable definition was agreed upon. The response of the opponent was usually to marvel at Socrates' wisdom, rather than take umbrage at his verbal trickery. Here one must allow not only for the good manners of the Greeks, but also for the fact that Socrates left no written work – his thoughts come to us via the dialogues of his brilliant pupil Plato.

Once the interlocutor tripped himself up, there was no going back because Socrates never allowed his interlocutors to accept a point provisionally or to argue cases in which they did not believe. According to Socrates himself, this was because his method had a moral element. He was concerned not with what men *might* think, but with what they actually did think. The objective of philosophy is to improve men's souls and not merely refine a disembodied canon of thought. More practically, Socrates wanted to prevent his opponents from reciting pre-prepared answers which they had learned verbatim from so-called experts. 'A book,' he said, 'can answer no questions.' The two rationales are really one and the same, for Socrates wanted men to think for themselves (if only because that is the only state in which they are malleable enough to be convinced by his arguments). While the Socratic method seeks to discover how humans *per se* ought to live, it is also concerned with impressing on individuals the correct fashion in which to conduct their lives.

Every thinking person periodically questions their aims and motives and the beliefs that underpin them. The kind of interrogation practised by Socrates was directed towards the most general kinds of truth, the 'bigger picture' as it were. In everyday life, however, questioning the grounds of our entire world-view does not tend to yield practical advice. Arriving at a picture of what we are and where we should be going is a piecemeal process, and any changes to our lives are made on the basis of what has gone before. If, for example, I ask a friend's advice on how to present myself at a job interview, I want to be told to buy a new tie or get myself a smart haircut. I do not want to hear that I should change my entire wardrobe or consider a different career. On the other hand, the reasoning behind Socratic method is that a truly accurate view of the world is one that does not harbour the inconsistencies which questioning by Socrates reveals. If we find a perfectly consistent standpoint, then we have found the truth. We may no longer believe that there can be only one 'correct' world-view, and most of us accept that a certain degree of inconsistency in one's beliefs is less a sign of ignorance than a reflection of a world in which absolute truths cannot be guaranteed. However, if my interview is for a job at an old-fashioned insurance company and my personal style favours shoulder-length hair and facial piercings, consistency requires that I either alter my appearance radically or seek employment elsewhere. To expect to succeed otherwise is at the very least to display a somewhat unbalanced view of the world.

The Athenians' desire to better themselves eventually ran out with their patience. Consisting as it did in the public humiliation of the great and the good, Socrates' search for the truth was quite correctly identified as undermining the fabric of Greek society. Noblemen such as Critias and Charmides had been shown not to know what temperance or moderation were. The great generals Laches and Nicias had been revealed to be ignorant of the meaning of courage. Finally, Socrates denigrated the essential principle of Athenian democracy by arguing that decisions should not be made by vote, but by philosopher kings on the basis of their superior wisdom. It was only through this means, he held, that we could avoid the iniquities of mob rule and leaders who pander to the worst passions of their electorate. In another, less commendable sense, his stance is reminiscent of that taken by American and European communists during the Cold War. By denouncing the Western model of democracy, they criticized the very system that allowed such protest to take place. The McCarthy trials aside, the authorities of Athens were not as forgiving as our own. Socrates was charged with corrupting the young and sentenced to death by poisoning. As the hemlock took hold, his friends gathered around to strain for his last words of wisdom. 'We owe a cock to Aesculapius,' he croaked, 'do not forget to pay the debt.'

5 | Plato's Cave
The use of analogy and allegory

In June 1998, the US Department of Justice filed a lawsuit against the Microsoft Corporation, arguing that its decision to include an internet browser in the new Windows 98 PC operating system was in breach of laws banning anti-competitive practices. In the *Wall Street Journal* on 10 November 1997, the CEO of Microsoft, Bill Gates, used a widely reported analogy to explain why his company should not be forced to remove the feature: 'I doubt the *New York Times* would let a newsstand tear out the business section of the paper just because it wanted to sell more *Wall Street Journals*. Or that the Ford Motor Company would let its dealers replace a Ford engine with a Toyota engine.'

The question is whether Mr Gates was making a fair comparison. In the opinion of the Department of Justice, he was not. The measures he imagined are not applied to newspapers and automobiles because no one company has a virtual monopoly in those industries. To tear pages out of the *Wall Street Journal* would hamper its ability to compete with rivals. The entire point of the anti-trust suit brought against Gates's company, on the other hand, was that the free bundling of a browser with its software prevented other browser makers from competing with Microsoft. The analogy does not stand up to a closer examination of the facts, even though it sounds at first hearing to be a fair point. Sometimes it is easy to be seduced by an elegant simile that compares one thing to another erroneously. The fact that something sounds apposite does not, of course, make it true. For this reason the Western philosophical tradition – not to mention the legal system – has emphasized the importance of logical arguments over analogies, relegating the latter to a chiefly illustrative role. The idea is that if something can be adequately demonstrated using logic and the facts at hand, there would be no need for analogies.

When literal explanations fail to convince, philosophers resort to analogies, allegories and metaphors. Sometimes this is because an apposite simile can get a point across more quickly and easily. If, for this purpose, a picture is worth a thousand words, then an analogy can be worth as many arguments. For example, the notion that our thoughts and emotions can be explained with reference to the workings of our brains is one of the most cogently argued yet intuitively unconvincing theories of philosophy today. No matter how strong the case that consciousness is a product of the brain instead of, say, an immaterial soul, it is still puzzling how intangible thoughts and emotions can be formed by the decidedly material contents of the skull. This may be because we are using the wrong image rather than the wrong idea. If we think of the brain churning out thoughts like a machine manufacturing widgets, we are bound to ask how its products can be so unlike the appliance that created them. Things become clearer if we imagine the brain to work rather like a special kind of machine: a computer. The American philosopher Hilary Putnam (1926–) has suggested that brains are the 'hardware' that run the 'software' of consciousness, just as PCs are the hardware that run computer programs. This analogy does not by itself prove anything – it remains to be shown whether or not brains really do function in this way – but it gives us a better understanding of how an otherwise unintelligible process might work.

At best, however, similes are more than just aids to understanding. The word analogy, or *analogia*, originally meant equality of ratios or proportion. When we use analogies to support a case, we take two things or processes which, though different, share a common structure, form or other characteristics. Having linked them together in this way, we then take a further quality possessed by the first thing and infer that the second thing also possesses it by virtue of what other features the two things share. For example, the English philosopher and Anglican priest William Paley (1743–1805) attempted to prove God's existence by drawing attention to the beauty and order exhibited in the natural world. So intricate is nature, he maintained, that it evinces the hand of a designer. At the core of Paley's argument was his famous watch analogy. If you were to come across a watch lying on a beach, you would not take it for a strange kind of pebble that had been washed up – for nothing of the kind could have formed by chance. You would infer that it had certainly been created by a watchmaker. Since the processes of nature display an equal complexity and precision, they too imply an artificer. Such inferences will never be infallible, as they involve speculating about matters we have not directly witnessed. Assuming that we can accept this, we may at least allow analogies to point us in the direction of where to look for our answers. Paley's analogy was a compelling one and demanded a serious response from his opponents. Admittedly, one could open a watch's casing and look for the inscription 'Made in Switzerland', whereas the trademark of heaven is not so readily discernible in the natural world. Nevertheless, the order manifest in the latter is as striking as that of any mechanical construct and is just as unlikely to have arisen through pure happenstance. Because of this equivalence, an explanation of the apparent 'design' in nature is required, whether or not one looks to God for it. In the event, Charles Darwin (1809–82) was later able to show that the complexity of the earth's species could have arisen without the conscious intervention of a deity – through evolution by natural selection. Richard Dawkins (1941–), the evolutionary biologist and subject of a later chapter in this book, titled a book on this process *The Blind Watchmaker*.

If natural selection had been discovered before watches were invented, then we might have concluded that the timepiece found on the beach had evolved in the same way as animals and plants. We could imagine a sceptic denying the existence of craftsmen skilled enough to produce it. 'Since a conscious intelligence was not involved in the creation of men and beasts,' he or she would say, 'neither should we imagine one to have fashioned this strange metallic object.' What this shows is that the conclusions we draw from analogies must be treated as provisional. They should be regarded as the starting point for further investigation rather than as the end of it.

In philosophy, the use of analogies to prove a point on the one hand and to merely elucidate one on the other has often been blurred. Plato's dialogues are among the most readable works of philosophy in the canon, and this is partly because they are so rich in similes and metaphors. Born in 428 BC, Plato was the youngest son in a rich and famous Athenian family. His real name was said to be Aristocles – 'Plato', or 'Platon', being a nickname derived from the breadth of either his shoulders or his forehead. As a youth, he received the standard education enjoyed by young aristocrats and become a champion wrestler as well as a skilled musician and poet. Well suited to the physical life, he served in the Athenian military between 409 BC and 404 BC at the close of the Peloponnesian war with Sparta. After the war he joined the cause of the Thirty Tyrants, the oligarchy established in Athens in 404 BC. Though one of its leaders was his uncle Charmides, the violence committed by this group soon prompted Plato to leave. By the time democracy was restored a year later, Plato had given up his political ambitions. This decision was confirmed by the execution of his teacher Socrates in 399 BC, after which Plato travelled in Egypt, Italy and Sicily. This was followed by another stint in the army, during which he was reputed to have been decorated for bravery in battle. Concluding that his political influence would come from instruction rather than example, in 387 BC he founded the Academy, a school of learning devoted to science and philosophy, that convened in the grove of

Academos. The school was intended to be a breeding ground for future statesmen who, Plato hoped, would do a better job than their predecessors. Though its founder died at the age of eighty, the Academy lasted for almost nine centuries until it was condemned as a pagan establishment and closed down by the Christian emperor Justinian. Plato did have one opportunity for a more direct influence upon his times. When the ruler of Syracuse, Dionysius I, died, Plato accepted, somewhat against his better judgement, the offer of the former ruler's brother-in-law, Dion, to tutor Dionysius II. The plan fell apart when the new ruler exiled Dion from Syracuse. Plato was imprisoned and subsequently sold into slavery, from which he had to be ransomed by a friend.

After his first meeting with the great Socrates in 408 BC, when he was twenty, Plato publicly burned the verses he had written and vowed to pursue a life of philosophy. To prove his dedication, he once claimed that he had chosen to live in a street occupied by goldsmiths so that when sleepiness began to overcome his thoughts he would be awoken by the noise of their tools. He soon became Socrates' most able pupil, taking up the ideas of his teacher and elaborating upon them at length in his dialogues. Plato does not himself feature in these dialogues, and since Socrates is always their protagonist it is sometimes difficult to discern whether the views expressed in them belong to the master or the pupil. There is some evidence that Socrates was bemused by how Plato represented him, and he once had a dream in which his protégé turned into a crow before jumping on to his head and pecking at his bald spot. The view of the consensus is that the theory of Forms that underpins many of the arguments in Plato's dialogues belongs chiefly to Plato rather than Socrates. This theory, according to which the physical world of images and impressions is a pale imitation of a higher world of knowledge and truth, draws on the principle of analogy. Under its terms we cannot know things such as trees and animals, since the world of appearances they populate is not worthy of knowledge proper. In Plato's view, we can only truly know that which is truly real, and this criterion is met solely by perfect and unchanging objects. Somewhere, he held, there resides an ideal tree that makes the grade, and it is from this one that ordinary trees derive their form. It is also the object which our everyday talk of trees hints at. When it comes to the ordinary oaks and sycamores of parks and woodlands, we have a relation to them which is inferior but analogous to knowledge – that is, we merely perceive them. We can, however – with the right philosophical training – acquire knowledge of the counterparts of trees and animals that reside in the world of eternal truth. Whereas perceptions can be blurred or mistaken, any knowledge of this higher realm would be perfect and never subject to revision.

Plato describes our relationship to the world of truth using one of the most famous analogies in Western philosophy: the simile of the cave. In his masterpiece *The Republic*, Plato asks us to imagine that there are men imprisoned in a cave who have never seen the outside world. They are held in chains with their backs to the entrance and cannot move even their heads to turn and see each other or the daylight behind. A fire is kept burning outside the low opening to the cave and people who pass before this fire cast shadows of themselves and their burdens on to the wall before the prisoners. If one of the passers-by should speak, then the sound would echo off that wall and the prisoners would naturally assume that the words they heard were uttered by the shadows. As they have been in this predicament from birth, the prisoners deem reality to be nothing more than this display of flickering shadows. Now, if one of these men was suddenly released from his fetters and made to turn around and face the light, his eyes would be dazzled and hurt by the fire and the daylight. Since he is unac- customed to light, he would not be able to see those walking past the cave's entrance clearly and would not immediately believe that he was looking at a world more 'real' than the one he had grown up in. He would need first to look at dimmer things such as stars in the night sky and reflections in water before progressing to behold objects in full daylight. Eventually, he would be able to look at the sun itself and realize that it is this that determines the seasons and makes his perceptions possible. Plato's cave is often compared today to a movie theatre from which we emerge blinking and unsteady after a matinee.

It is paradoxical that while Plato wishes to dismiss ordinary beliefs about everyday objects as merely analogous to knowledge of ideal ones, the parable of the cave in which he makes this point most vividly is itself an analogy. This may seem self-contradictory, but we need to remember that the value of a good simile lies not in how it can prove a case so much as in the way it can point us in the general direction of the truth. By using the method of allegory, Plato's cave helps to lead us from well-trodden ground into the unfamiliar territory where, he hopes, the analogy will no longer be needed. The story also explains why Plato's ideas, presented as those of Socrates, might not immediately convince his listeners, for if the former prisoner should return to the cave and inform those still captive of the world outside they would deride him as a crank. Many thinkers in the real world who attempted to see the truth behind appearances have met with a similar response. When Galileo directed his telescope upon Jupiter, he discovered the planet's moons and found that one celestial body can orbit another even though it is not the centre of the universe. He reasoned by analogy that the earth itself could lie in a similar arrangement. Widely dismissed as ridiculous at the time, his reasoning none the less helped lead to the modern understanding of the solar system.

The sun is of crucial importance in Plato's story. Plato denied that knowledge was equivalent to perception, for perception was unreliable whereas true knowledge should be infallible. However, his analogy of the soul with the eye shows that he thought that knowledge works by a similar mechanism to perception. For Plato, apprehension is *of* something *by* something *via* something. There must be an apprehender, something that is apprehended, and finally a medium through which the apprehension takes place. Just as the sun is the cause of our perceptions through the light it emits, there is something that is the cause of knowledge through a kind of intellectual light that operates on the soul. Plato called this thing the idea of the 'Good', which is the source of truth and reason in men and women. It was the task of philosophy to teach us to use reason – our intellectual 'eye' – properly, directing it upon things that at first may be difficult or even painful to regard. The cave and the sun work both as allegories and arguments for Plato. Firstly, they tell us a story of how we come to be blind to the truth and how we might come to see the light. Secondly, if we accept that the ability to understand is a faculty like the ability to see or hear, then it will require a medium just as sight requires light as a medium. When this factor is absent – and the light of reason is eschewed in favour of faith or fancy – then we will be truly in the dark as far as knowledge is concerned.

This makes Plato's view sound rather sober, but at the same time he believed that the idea of the 'Good' – the object that emitted intellectual 'light' – was as real as the sun (more real, in fact, since it was located in the eternal and unchanging realm of ideas). Most adults would require more evidence than a mere analogy before they started to believe in such an occult entity. Knowledge resembles perception – or sight, at least – in many ways, but it does not seem to require an other-worldly power source for its operation. Neither, for that matter, do *all* the senses require a medium. Sight requires a light source, while hearing depends upon air to carry sounds, but there does not seem to be an equivalent in the case of touch, for example, where all that is needed are hands and objects. Moreover, the sun is not the only source of light. Since lamps, torches and candles can all provide the illumination that enables us to see, the 'light' of understanding itself might have more than one source rather than the 'Good' alone. Just as the discovery of conflicting facts can sink a theory, conflicting images like these can put paid to an analogy. While Plato's simile impels us to investigate the 'Good' further, equally powerful disanalogies tell us not to bother.

The light of the sun and the 'light' of reason make for a pleasing comparison, and it is not surprising that Plato was seduced. Arguments from analogy seek to show that two things similar in one way must be similar in another way also. When we say this, we think that the traits we have already found to be similar are the essential ones – the ones that determine whether or not an object will have those extra characteristics that are the subject of the investigation. What we human beings deem essential, however, nature may have other ideas about, and this is often why arguments from analogy fail. For example, while nature may allow one kind of berry to be nutritious, this does not bar her from creating other varieties that are poisonous though they look similar. Toxicity may be a very important issue for us, but it seems to be less so for plants, which do not take care to look succulent only when they are edible to humans. Appearances do serve as a useful guide for foragers, as by close inspection – accompanied by a little knowledge – one can usually tell a blackberry bush from deadly nightshade. Yet even experts are sometimes mistaken, and it would be foolhardy to expect every small, black and shiny fruit to taste delicious.

As we have seen, analogies work to suggest lines of future investigation into facts concerning the natural world rather than to demonstrate such truths themselves. Sometimes, however, they function as more than signposts to truth. This happens when we have already decided what the truth is but are unaware of its ramifications, as often happens in the realm of morality. The notion of animal rights, for example, is founded on the analogies that can be drawn between human beings and other living creatures. A chimpanzee has the cognitive abilities of a human infant. Therefore, animal rights activists argue, a chimpanzee should have the same rights as we confer on children and, by extension, the same rights to life as adults enjoy. In this case, we have decided what an individual must possess in order to demand rights. If it is the ability to demonstrate consciousness of some sort and a sensitivity to pain, then at least the 'higher' animals qualify as well as people. Admittedly, the mental faculties of an ape or dolphin are limited and do not develop beyond those of a human child, but neither do those of severely handicapped adults and we do not relegate their status to that of animals. On the contrary, many societies today arguably take greater care to protect the rights of the disabled than those of citizens who can fend for themselves. We therefore employ double standards when we deny rights to animals.

Analogies are very effective at exposing such irregularities on our part. The physical world operates according to its own laws, but when it comes to ethics it is we who are in charge. If we say that cognitive abilities confer the right to life then that is a decision we have taken, not a fact that we may or may not have discovered. Arguments from analogy in the moral realm consequently call upon us to be fair and consistent in our decision-making. Nature, on the other hand, while certainly unfair, is beyond our control and cannot be expected to be consistent.

6 | Aristotle's Goals
The purposes of life

Aristotle did not a have a single method which he applied to all his philosophy. He thought that each area of study had its own procedures of inquiry and standards of exactitude. As he wrote of ethics,

Our discussion will be adequate if it has as much clearness as the subject-matter admits of, for precision is not to be sought for all alike in all discussions, any more than in all the products of the crafts.

Nevertheless, Aristotle did have an idea that he thought could help explain many things, from the movement of heavenly bodies to the behaviour of human beings: teleology. This was the notion that the present could be understood by reference to the future. The nature of a thing – be it an acorn or a man – was inextricably linked to its *telos*, its goal or final end. The final end of an object informs its nature, and that nature subsequently drives it towards its goal. The goal of an acorn, for example, is an oak tree, and we can only understand the acorn by reference to what it has the potential to become. Acorns, moreover, only ever grow into oaks, never into firs or apple trees, yet they are nourished by the same water and soil as these other species. According to Aristotle it was the acorn's *telos*, expressed in its constitution, that made the difference. Human beings too had a final end and, if we could understand what it was, we would be all the better equipped to achieve it.

Aristotle was born in Stagira, a small Greek colony on the Thracian coast, in 384 BC. His father, who died when Aristotle was a boy, was court physician to the King of Macedonia, hence the philosopher's long connection with that state. When he was eighteen, he travelled to Athens to study at the Academy under Plato. There he remained for the next twenty years, emerging as his master's outstanding, though not always most obedient, student. He might have been expected to take over the school after Plato's death in 347 BC, but as a resident alien he was legally barred from owning Athenian property. In any case, Aristotle's views had by then radically diverged from Platonic orthodoxy. 'Plato is dear to me,' he said, 'but dearer still is truth.' Unlike his teacher, he preferred investigating facts to speculating over lofty ideals, at least in the first instance. Plato's nephew, Speusippus, assumed charge of the Academy, while Aristotle left to travel in Asia Minor with his friends and colleagues Theophrastes and Xenocrates. There he married Pythias, the niece of the ruler of Atarneus, but two years after her uncle was murdered in a rebellion he was summoned to the Macedonian capital, Pella, by King Philip. The king asked Aristotle, as the world's greatest intellectual, to tutor his thirteen-year-old son, the future Alexander the Great. This was a task the philosopher relished, for, unlike Plato, he believed that this back-room role was the proper station of philosophers. As he writes in a surviving fragment of his lost work, *On Kingship*:

It is not merely unnecessary for a king to be a philosopher, but even a disadvantage. Rather a king should take the advice of true philosophers. Then he would fill his reign with good deeds, not with good words.

Whether or not Alexander's deeds could be described as 'good', he at least managed to conquer the known world. Aristotle seems to have had little influence on his charge beyond instilling dreams of Homeric glory in the boy. For example, he once advised Alexander that the best way to keep the defeated barbarians servile to the Greeks was to resist intermarriage. His pupil responded by marrying the daughter of a Persian nobleman and forcing his generals to act likewise. Aristotle nevertheless remained Alexander's informal, and often distant, adviser when he came of age, only incurring displeasure when the emperor felt moved to execute his chronicler – and Aristotle's blood nephew – Callisthenes of Olynthus for treason in 328 BC.

Aristotle withdrew to the family property in Stagira after three years at the Macedonian court, and then returned to Athens in 335 BC when he was nearing fifty. Speusippus had died by this time and Aristotle's old friend, Xenocrates, was elected the new head of the Academy. Aristotle established a rival school called the Lyceum in a grove outside the city. Over the next thirteen years, he gave advanced talks to an inner circle of pupils before delivering lectures to a wider audience in the evenings. Many of the philosopher's surviving works date from this time, largely in the form of lecture notes. These number forty-seven volumes, but probably represent little more than a quarter of his total output. He was the greatest expert of his day in every intellectual field, from astronomy and logic to anatomy and geography. No individual, before or since, has ever matched this. His downfall came in 323 BC, when the death of Alexander the Great prompted a revolt against the pro-Macedonian government of Athens. As an associate of the late emperor, Aristotle faced trumped-up charges of impiety. He fled so that, as he was reported to have said, 'The Athenians might not have another opportunity of sinning against philosophy as they had already done with Socrates.' A year later, he succumbed to a stomach illness and died where he took refuge, on the Mediterranean island of Euboea.

The question of 'final ends' was a small, though persistent, part of Aristotle's voluminous work. He argued that the scientists who had preceded him, such as Democritus (460–370 BC), had concentrated too much on the 'push' of the past and not enough on the 'pull' of what was to come. He explained that there were four distinct causes of things – material, formal, efficient and final. The material cause of a statue, for example, would be the marble or bronze out of which it was made. This matter held the potentiality of the statue in its lumpen mass. The formal cause was the idea or image according to which it was fashioned. This existed as a plan in the mind of the sculptor. The sculptor is also the efficient cause – that is, the agent of the change that the marble or bronze undergoes. The 'final' cause is the purpose for which the statue was made, such as the desire to please a patron or earn a living as an artist. According to Aristotle, all action involves the releasing of one or other kind of potentiality in matter with this final cause in sight. The egg is potentially the chicken and, after incubation, achieves its end in hatching. Water, meanwhile, holds the potentiality of steam, which is released through the agency of a fire placed beneath the cauldron. All things strive to move from potentiality to their actuality, and ultimately to a state of perfection, which is also a state of rest. Motion and change are the means by which they get there, directed by their final causes, or goals. Stones, for instance, fall to the ground when we drop them rather than floating up into the clouds because they are essentially material things and strive for the earth, which is the lowest place. Flames, on the other hand, have something of the heavens about them and shoot upwards. Other objects seek out different resting places according to their own particular nature.

Whereas the final end of a statue requires the agency of the sculptor to release its potentiality, natural objects contain within themselves their own agency. Everything in the natural world, Aristotle thought, had a *telos* and exhibited a natural design to seek it out. Flames and stones too have a *telos*, but it was the designs offered by zoological study that provided Aristotle with his clearest illustrations. He was struck by how so much in the living world seemed arranged not haphazardly, but purposefully and in the most complicated and improbable ways. It is the purpose of eyes, for example, to see, and they are put together with such complexity that sight becomes possible. It is the purpose of cheetahs to hunt gazelles, for which they are granted strong legs for running after their prey. Gazelles, for their part, strive for the goal of eluding cheetahs, and so they too can run very quickly. Both animals, along with human beings, have incisor teeth for biting and molars for chewing, tasks for which they are respectively well suited. Left to chance, we might sometimes be born with molars at the front of our mouths and incisors at the back. Why this so rarely happens is to be explained by the hand of purpose, though Aristotle did not think that this hand needed to be attached to the arm of an intelligent Creator. The notion of a universe designed for our benefit by a benevolent God was an adaptation of Aristotle's thought on the part of his Christian commentators. The god envisaged by Aristotle enjoyed a condition of absolute actuality and perfect rest. All of his work – all of his potentiality – was achieved, so to speak, and He was unlikely to be concerned with the affairs of mortals.

Aristotle was right that such characteristics as sharp teeth and strong legs do not achieve ubiquity in a species through chance. He was unaware, however, of the mechanism of natural selection that brings them about – a factor that would remain unknown until the publication of Darwin's *Origin of Species* in 1859. The cheetahs born with weak legs would have starved to death before they could pass their traits on to their progeny, and so would eventually have been outbred by their strong-legged rivals. Neither were those legs something that the cheetah species 'sought out', as it were, as a final end, for they were only a response to their environment – in this case, the speed of their prey. Had gazelles evolved sharp teeth and claws to defend themselves instead of strong legs with which to flee, more powerfully built cheetahs would predominate over the lean specimens 'designed' for speed. This scenario might even come to pass if we wait another few thousand years. It is easy to see why speed is such a successful trait in the gene pool at present, as it helps cheetahs to achieve their aim of catching prey. But that aim is not, strictly speaking, the aim of their legs. Similarly, eyes are not 'for' seeing, they simply *see* – an ability that ensures their proliferation in the gene pool. Natural selection is not the inherent process by which nature moves from potentiality to actuality, to use Aristotle's terminology. Rather, it is a 'blind' mechanism that does not favour one final end over another. All it ensures is that those traits better suited to a particular environment proliferate – and that environment can change, as it did for the trilobite and the dinosaur and may, one day, for us too.

Teleology – the language of purpose – is anathema to the modern evolutionary biologist. Long before Darwin and Mendel (1822–84), it was jettisoned from physics by the scientists who looked instead for efficient causes – the kind that precede an event and act to bring it about. A falling stone may be pulled towards the ground, for example, but this is due to the force of gravity acting upon it. The English twentieth-century philosopher Bertrand Russell (1872–1970) wrote: 'Ever since the beginning of the seventeenth century, almost every serious intellectual advance has had to begin with an attack on some Aristotelian doctrine.' Yet no less a figure than Charles Darwin acknowledged Aristotle to have been the greatest ever contributor to the understanding of biology. Unfortunately, the methods Aristotle expounded were not employed by his heirs. Admitting, in *On the Generation of Animals*, that he did not know how bees developed into adulthood, Aristotle wrote:

The facts have not yet been sufficiently established. If they ever are, then credit must be given to observation rather than to theories, and to theories only insofar as they are confirmed by the observed facts.

For the better part of two thousand years after Aristotle's death, philosophers largely gave up observing facts. Research was, for the most part, limited to observing Aristotle instead. The

Church was instrumental in entrenching Aristotle's thoughts and discouraged fresh investigation as a form of impiety. The Elizabethan philosopher Sir Francis Bacon (1561–1626) told a story of how a group of monks met in the Middle Ages to discuss how many teeth a horse had. Unable to find the answer in any of Aristotle's works, one of the younger and more naive among them suggested that they should retire to the stable and count. For this he was expelled from the meeting. The anecdote says less about the errors of Aristotle than about those who retained his conclusions while eschewing his painstaking methods. Recent commentators have been less severe on the philosopher than those of a century past, perhaps because so many of the dogmas that Aristotle inspired have now been expunged. We are kinder to our enemies once they have been defeated. That said, Aristotle's teleological thought has not been overturned as comprehensively as it might seem. In biology we cannot understand the construction and development of eyes and other organs unless we know the uses to which they are put. Most importantly, whether or not eyes are *for* seeing or simply *see*, denying them their natural function certainly leads to their decay. The eyes of a man long imprisoned in a dark cave will be unable to focus in the sunlight once he is released, just as his teeth will eventually weaken and fall out if he is fed only on fluids.

The same analysis applies to man's function as a living being. Aristotle viewed moral depravity as a dereliction of our function, a denial of our essence and final end. A good individual, on the other hand, is one who carries out his function well, rather as a good knife is one that cuts well. But how do we discover what man's function is? Aristotle defined it as that part of our nature that is exclusive to humans. It cannot, then, be the faculty of growth, for we share this with plants. Nor can it be that of sensation, because this is also possessed by animals. Those who live with pleasure as their only goal are behaving as mere beasts do. What we do have that no other creature has, however, is the faculty of reason. Just as we cannot understand a knife unless we know that its function is to cut, or an acorn unless we know that its end is to grow into an oak tree, we do not understand ourselves unless we are appraised of the faculty that is particular to us and the goal that it makes possible for us to achieve. This goal – the final end to which all our other ends are merely means – is *eudaimonia*, or happiness we might say. To Aristotle, *eudaimonia* consists in acting in accordance with reason. One form of rational activity is practical reasoning – the kind involved in moral virtues such as courage and generosity. The purpose of one's life is to be good – to be *good at* being human. Yet even though a person exhibits all the moral virtues to the right degree, misfortune might still contrive to cause them unhappiness. The truly happy individual will also need to be healthy, wealthy and not a slave (or a woman), Aristotle believed.

Fortunately, Aristotle added, there is another kind of reasoning that is immune to the vicissitudes of life. The intellectual faculties are the most exalted facet of man and they deliver an even higher form of happiness than moral virtue: the activity of philosophical contemplation. We could not engage in this all day long (since we have to eat) but, while we do, we are exercising the finest element of ourselves and the one that, according to Aristotle, we share with the gods. This may seem a surprising conclusion, as too much philosophy is commonly thought to make one miserable. It did not have this effect on Aristotle himself who was, by all accounts, a cheerful individual, but this is beside the point. 'Happiness' is only a rough translation of what Aristotle termed *eudaimonia*, which is quite different from contentment. *Eudaimonia* is not a sedentary state that we achieve at the end of acting well, like a reward. Our final end is itself a form of activity and the good life consists in its execution, just as we might visit a restaurant in order to enjoy a good dinner without expecting the latter to be something we receive after the dessert course.

Eudaimonia, while difficult to attain, is far less elusive than 'happiness'. I may have a large house, two cars, a good job and a wonderful family, yet still ask myself 'Am I happy?' There can be less doubt whether one has achieved *eudaimonia* for it is measured by objective facts rather than subjective feelings. In Aristotle's view, for as long as one exercises intellectual virtue unmolested the highest form of human life has been achieved.

7 | Lucretius's Spear
The realm of the hypothetical

Titus Lucretius Carus was the Latin poet who wrote the philosophical poem, *On the Nature of Things*. Born around 94 BC, little is known of him aside from his most famous work. Before he was driven insane by a love potion and committed suicide in 55 BC, he devised a test by which we could tell whether the universe was finite or infinite without having to travel all the way to its boundaries for a tour of inspection. Supposing that there was an end to the universe, Lucretius asked, what would happen if someone went there, to the very edge, and hurled a spear. One of two things: either the spear would continue onward, or it would rebound. Whichever way, it would mean that there was something beyond the edge of the universe – either an object to get in the spear's way or more space for it to travel through. Therefore, he concluded, space cannot have a boundary and must be infinite.

Lucretius was conducting a thought experiment, which differs from the kind of experiments scientists conduct in that it takes place in the head rather than in the laboratory. Like laboratory experiments, the philosophical kind seek to isolate the quality we wish to investigate. To find out, for example, whether cellphones cause damage to brain cells, researchers will bear in mind that many other factors can also cause damage – such as natural ageing, trauma or alcohol abuse. If they are to prove that cellphones are dangerous (or completely harmless) they will need to ensure that these other factors do not have the chance to inflict any more damage than normal during the course of the test. Thought experiments, or hypothetical scenarios, function in much the same way – isolating the crucial variables to see what happens when one thing changes while everything else stays the same. Isolation, however, can do strange things to ideas.

In the Jack Lemmon comedy *Under the Yum Yum Tree* (1963), Robin and David – a prospective bride and groom – are beginning to doubt the durability of their union. Unsure whether they are truly in love, the bride-to-be concocts a simple means of settling the matter: they are to abstain from sex for a period and see if they can still sustain their relationship. What is being put to the test here is an absolute claim: that true love can survive any deprivation – including separate beds. The couple reason that if they cannot get along in such an arrangement, then they cannot be truly in love with each other. Lemmon, their landlord (who, unbeknownst to the groom, has his own designs on Robin) counsels David on how to lower his libido. As Lemmon's scheme unfolds, however, the lovers' squabbling illustrates not the foresightedness of their doubts, but rather, one of the potential pitfalls in such experiments. A more helpful test of their fidelity might have been to live exactly as they would when married. By keeping sex out of the experiment, they altered the nature of the very thing they were trying to put to the test – their relationship. The young couple would have been better advised to spend a longer period living together instead of flitting between each other's rooms if they wished to allay – or confirm – their worries. In the event, all they succeeded in testing was their tolerance for celibacy.

Love often finds itself the subject of such experiments, though, unlike Lemmon's couple, we usually confine them to our imagination. Unsure of our feelings, we mull over questions such as 'Will I still love her in twenty years? If he were old and grey? If she were the victim of a terrible accident?' Such thoughts are fine within limits, but considering hypothetical situations like these can leave us wondering whether we have changed the variables of our relationship with someone or are no longer talking about the same person. It is clearly pointless to ask whether we would still love someone if they became an entirely different person. At the same time, we commonly feel that true love must allow for changes of circumstance. The difficulty is knowing when we have tested a concept to breaking point before it is twisted out of all recognition.

The problem is a pertinent one for philosophers because they deal in generalities and universals – and if any proposition or theory is to be universally valid then it must be shown to hold even under outlandish conditions. Outlandish conditions are particularly prevalent in philosophical discussions of personal identity – that is, the question of whether there is a self that persists through time and makes the fifty-year-old Julie Smith the *same person* as the infant Julie Smith we see in the family album. Philosophers sometimes face the accusation that they are merely frustrated scientists. A study of recent literature regarding personal identity, on the other hand, yields the slightly different conclusion that they are frustrated science-fiction writers. Where the subjects in philosophers' thought experiments used to do nothing more strenuous than travel on the 'Clapham omnibus', they are today likely to find themselves teleported through space, fissioning like an amoeba or undergoing head transplants.

The debate about personal identity begins with the ancient story of the Ship of Theseus. During this vessel's long voyage, its damaged timbers were replaced one by one. Eventually, the ship returned from sea possessing none of the original timbers with which it was launched. The question is then asked: is it the same ship as the one that began the voyage? Given that the process of change was gradual, we are normally inclined to say that the historical relationship of the two ships is sufficient to judge that they are one and the same. This 'continuity' account of identity can be thrown into confusion by a simple hypothetical counter-example. What would we say if the ship had been shadowed throughout its voyage by another vessel crewed by carpenters who collected the discarded timbers and used them to build an exact replica of the ship? There is now a rival for the title of the Ship of Theseus, and this new contender has a strong claim as it is composed of the very same pieces of wood as the vessel that left the harbour many years earlier. It does not matter that this third ship might exist only in our imagination – the fact that it is possible means that we must consider it. The replica ship presents a worthy counter-example against the continuity theory of identity precisely because the essential nature of the returning Ship of Theseus has not been altered in any way by its acquiring a *doppelgänger*. We have merely brought in a third party that changes the variables of its situation.

The picture is not always so clear. A number of people have been able to lead relatively normal lives despite suffering catastrophic injuries that have left them with only one functioning brain hemisphere. In a futuristic turn on these cases, the English philosopher David Wiggins (1933–) asked what would happen to his self if his brain was divided into two hemispheres that were then transplanted into two different bodies. Wiggins's question challenges anyone who believes the brain to be the house of the self. Imagine you fell victim to a disease that destroyed your body and one of your brain's hemispheres. Since we are in the future, the technology exists to save the remaining hemisphere and transplant it into a new body. If you were to undergo the operation, then, given the record of past successes in this field, you might reasonably expect to wake up in the recovery room once it was all over. You may find yourself in an unfamiliar body, but it will nevertheless be you since the new body possesses your old brain. Your friends may find the change somewhat strange to begin with, but they will eventually get used to your new form. Now imagine a further twist: your surgeons tell you that they will in fact be able to save both hemispheres of your brain, only it will be necessary to separate them and implant them into different donor bodies.

Before the anaesthetic begins to work, you may have time to wonder which of the two bodies you will wake up in. One clearly cannot wake up in both bodies since that would involve being two people at once. It would also be strange if you did not wake up in either body. If the operation is deemed a success if only one hemisphere survives then how, Wiggins asks, could a 'double' success be deemed a failure? The statistic would not provide much comfort for the prospective patient.

While your self may survive the operation, our understanding of selfhood might not. We are used to thinking of the self as a unity, or at least believing that if we are identical with some older version of ourselves in the future, there will be only one such self at any given time. Wiggins, however, seems to show us that, at least in theory, the person who is Julie Smith in 2001 could be 'the same person as' two separate people in 2051. It transpires that it is not the patient's self that is being tested, but our concept of selfhood. We set out to discover the most extreme circumstances under which two individuals can be the same person, yet we have ended up altering the definition of what it means to be 'the same person'. We might reasonably object that Wiggins's hypothetical scenario is not concerned with what we commonly understand to be selfhood, and therefore has no bearing on ordinary notions of personal identity. Our everyday concepts were designed for everyday use and it is not their fault if they do not stand up to fanciful thought experiments dreamed up by philosophers. This would be a fair point to make if the scenario did not provoke a response in us and did not make us feel uncomfortable with our traditional conception of identity. To apply an ordinary concept – or any concept – only in contexts that are favourable to it is to put sentimentality before truth.

Since we are unlikely to find ourselves in the predicament Wiggins describes, we might not be unduly worried by letting his point pass. In the case of other concepts, such as love, we may not be so accommodating. Part of the problem with hypothetical scenarios is that it is often very difficult to tell where the variables end and the essential nature of the concept we are testing begins. In many cases there will be no clear line of division between the two. What we do know is that when we begin to think speculatively about matters close to our heart, it is easy to forget where we started. When we submit our love for someone to theoretical trials, we may not notice the spotlight passing from the beloved to a figment of our imagination. If we find that our feelings are contradicted in the face of something that exists only hypothetically, we would do well to make sure we have subjected those feelings to a fair examination. When a concept, belief or emotion fails a test we have prescribed for it, it is sometimes because – like Robin, David and Jack Lemmon – we have tested something quite different. Just as it would be unreasonable to blame the manu-facturers of an 'unbreakable' lock if a burglar should kick the entire door in, we should not expect one concept to fight the battles of another.

8 | Ockham's Razor
The virtues of simplicity

Faced with two philosophers discussing a complicated philosophical problem, a listener may be inclined to wonder what all the fuss is about. He might ask himself why they cannot just agree that the simplest explanation is the best one and then be done with it. This sentiment would in fact be echoed by most philosophers. The principle known as Ockham's Razor is named after William of Ockham, the medieval monk who wielded it so enthusiastically. Ockham famously advised that entities should not be multiplied beyond necessity. A formulation of the Razor agreeable to the modern scientist – not to mention the person of common sense – would be this: where two competing theories can both adequately explain a given phenomenon, the simpler of them is to be preferred.

Ockham was born in 1285 in either the Surrey village of Ockham or its namesake in Yorkshire. Little is known about his early life, but after training in the Franciscan order, he embarked on a course in theology at Oxford University. His controversial commentaries on Peter Lombard's *Sentences* – the standard religious textbook of the day – soon offended Oxford's theology faculty. Whereas St Augustine of Hippo (354–430 AD) regarded the Christian Sacraments as merely visible signs of the invisible grace of God, Lombard's account promoted them to actual causes of divine favour. Ockham, siding with the Augustinian view, would not accept that God required the participation of mortals in order to enact His will. After being denounced as a heretic, he was forced to leave the university without obtaining his master's degree. He completed his studies in Paris, where his views again provoked opposition and he was issued with a warning by the teaching authorities. Spotting a troublemaker, Pope John XXII summoned Ockham to Avignon, where he effectively imprisoned the monk in a convent for four years. Even there Ockham continued to court controversy, arguing that Franciscans should be allowed to renounce worldly goods. In 1328, Ockham fled to Munich with two other members of his order. For this act of defiance Pope John promptly issued his excommunication. In Munich, Ockham lived under the protection of the equally recalcitrant Emperor Louis IV, to whom he is supposed to have proposed, 'You defend me with the sword, and I will defend you with the pen.' He embroiled himself further in ecclesiastical politics and fervently supported the cause of the emperor in his power struggle with the papacy. Before eventually succumbing in 1349 to what was possibly the Black Death, Ockham found time to analyse John XXII's edicts thoroughly and – no doubt with great satisfaction – pronounced him a heretic and pseudo-pope.

It was admittedly for reasons other than simplicity that Ockham propounded his most famous thesis: that creatures and objects do not possess essences that exist independently. The prevailing view of the time (derived from Plato) was that in addition to Fido, Rover and all the other dogs, there also existed an object – 'Dog' – in whose image all our own dogs in their various shapes and sizes were made. If Dog cannot be found on this earth, then that does not matter because Dog, along with all essences, resides in the mind of the Creator where he happily chases 'Cat' and chews 'Bone'. Dispensing with these separately existing essences certainly makes for a simpler picture of the universe, but Ockham's real concern was that they would place a constraint on God's creative freedom. God, he argued, did not work from preconceived ideas when he fashioned the world, but carved as he pleased. Certain groups of objects, however, may still resemble one another in various ways, and this allows men to form universal concepts such as 'Man', 'Cat' and 'Oak Tree'. This is where the Razor comes in, for we can talk of these generalities without recourse to 'ideas in the mind of the Creator'. General terms, Ockham held, are symbols representing an 'intention' of the mind to group several ordinary objects together. Since there is no need to invoke an extra object – namely an essence of 'Oak Tree' to which the term would refer – there is indeed no such object. This view, known as 'nominalism', was Ockham's greatest theoretical achievement using the Razor. Unfortunately, Ockham did not stop there. He also used his Razor to dispense with the existence of motion – which can be described adequately, he held, by the reappearance of a thing in a different place. In this sense at least, Ockham may not be the best advertisement for his own principle.

In its purest form, the Razor is a working method rather than an insight into the nature of the world. As such, it cannot be refuted by an occasion where the simplest explanation is shown to be false. Since there is an indefinite number of possible hypotheses that can explain any set of facts, it saves time, if nothing else, to test the simplest hypothesis first. When, for example, someone repeatedly refuses your offer of a date, it could be because they have been exceptionally busy for the past six months, because they are too nervous to accept, or because you have not yet suggested an appealing venue. The simplest explanation, however – and the normal assumption in the circumstances – is to conclude that the person does not fancy you. Until they express feelings to the contrary, this position is advisable if you want to save your energy.

There is a further, more controversial, application that makes Ockham's Razor more than a mere rule of thumb. As the philosopher Ludwig Wittgenstein put it, 'A wheel which turns, though nothing turns with it, is not part of the mechanism.' In other words, wherever something is unnecessary for understanding a given process, there is a case for claiming that it plays no part in it. For example, behaviourist philosophers of the mind argue that our words and actions can be explained without talking about people's psychological experiences of intending, desiring and feeling. Without these entities an account of human action becomes much simpler, so, with a particularly ruthless stroke of Ockham's Razor, the behaviourists abolished them. As a result, they were accused of 'feigning anaesthesia' – of effectively denying the existence of consciousness. While the most bullish among them might accept the charge with pride, more moderate behaviourists argue that consciousness ('whatever that means') has no role to play in explaining how we act. In this way, the Razor is not necessarily a tool for dismissing those entities that have been multiplied beyond necessity, but merely a blade that cuts and separates entities so that they can be put in their proper place. For example, Darwinists believe that evolution accounts for our existence and that to cite the influence of God is to bring in a superfluous entity. They also protest that their aim is not to disprove the existence of God. They argue that although God may exist, He played no direct role in the creation of the human race. This relegation may or may not placate the religious. As ever when using the Razor, there is no guarantee that an entity's new status will not be as repugnant to its enthusiasts as its outright dismissal would have been.

One must take care to use Ockham's Razor only to prune the expendable elements of an explanatory theory – that is, those which do not do any useful work in explaining phenomena. It should not be used to slash away the very phenomena being explained (by breaking this rule, the theorist could make his job very easy indeed). Even the most extreme behaviourists are not guilty of this – they have not pruned our behaviour, as it were. They have, however, simplified their theory at the expense of another phenomenon worthy of consideration – the subjective nature of mental states such as imagining or feeling pain. The mental states they deny would demand explanation even if they do not play a role in behaviour. Their loss is a price too high to pay for simplicity.

We should note that Ockham's principle contains an implicit sub-clause: 'All other things being equal.' The simplest explanation is only to be preferred over a more complex one if their explanatory powers are otherwise equivalent. If a more complex theory can explain things far better than a simpler one, we should prefer the more complex theory. Ockham did not value simplicity above all else, he merely believed it gave us grounds for choosing between two equally adequate explanations. To the dismay of armchair historians, Ockham never used his Razor to solve a notorious but apocryphal scholastic conundrum: the question of how many angels can dance on the head of a pin. Using the Razor, the simplest answer, of course – and hence the 'correct' one – is but a single angel.

9 | Machiavelli's Prince
Appealing to our worse nature

Niccolò Machiavelli advised that, for the ruler, 'It is better to be feared than loved, more prudent to be cruel than compassionate.' Due to remarks like these, 'Machiavellian' has been a byword for villainy for centuries, but it more properly implies realism. The words 'fantasy' and 'idealism', on the other hand, have somehow avoided the opprobrium heaped on their rival, although on any fair account of twentieth-century history it is they that have more to answer for. The thoughts that made Machiavelli infamous were elucidated in *The Prince*, written in 1513 for Lorenzo de' Medici, the ruler of Florence. The book is nothing if not amoral. It is neither a discourse on the justification of state power nor a treatise on the moral aims that a ruler should pursue. On the contrary, it is a neutral guidebook for achieving and maintaining political power. Its strategies take men as they are, not as they might be. As Machiavelli wrote: 'The way men live is so far removed from the way they ought to live that anyone who abandons what is for what should be pursues his downfall rather than his preservation.' What use, after all, are political values without the power to put them into practice? The same sentiments are evident today in the vote-buying exploits of modern democratic politicians whenever Election Day looms. They may not admit to it, but their exploits too would find approval in the pages of *The Prince*.

Whereas many great philosophers have judged most people to be stupid, Machiavelli preferred to think of them as wicked. Rulers, he argued, were to assume the latter and only if they were lucky would they also be stupid. Admittedly, the wickedness he talked of was licentiousness and self-interest – two vices which modern liberalism and capitalism respectively tolerate. If Machiavelli's verdict on the behaviour of ordinary men and women seems harsh today, it would have sounded no less so in the philosophical climate of the early sixteenth century. The ethos of Renaissance humanism sought to liberate the virtuous intentions of mankind and allow them to inform the good running of the state. As a largely self-educated man, Machiavelli avoided such received ideas in his early studies. But while he rejected the emphasis his fellows placed on moral values, he shared the view of Galileo and others that man could come to understand God's design for the universe. His methodology was humanist even if his conclusions were not.

Books seem to have been Machiavelli's only entertainment in his youth. He was born into a relatively impoverished branch of an otherwise wealthy and powerful Florentine family in 1469. His unconventional learning did not hinder his professional progress and in 1498, when he was only twenty-nine, he was appointed a chancellor of Florence. Italy was beset by political turmoil at this time, with none of her four dominant city-states able to resist foreign influence. The last chapter of *The Prince* is entitled, 'Exhortation to Free Italy from the Barbarians', by which he meant the French and Spanish. Though Machiavelli wrote that their occupation 'stinks in the nostrils of us all', he saw how different life could be in a country united under a strong central ruler in 1500, when he spent five months at the French court on a diplomatic mission. Yet the citizens of France and Florence were not so unalike, he thought. They were all human beings with the same passions, and what succeeded for one race could be made to work for another. However, this could not be achieved by appealing to their better nature, he believed, for their supposed goodness was largely a fantasy. Rather, the most nefarious means a ruler can use to maintain his power are justified because his villainy is nothing compared to that of those he governs. Machiavelli even had a good word to say about the tyrannical Cesare Borgia, who carved a territory for himself in central Italy in a matter of months. Justification is not what primarily concerns Machiavelli. *The Prince* is a book of means rather than ends.

Machiavelli's precepts are admirably lucid and succinct – unlike, for example, the nebulous advice of today's guides to success in life and management. A ruler ideally wants to be both feared and loved – rather like God – but since usually only one of the two is possible at a given time, he or she should choose to be feared. This is the safer option, for people are

> . . . ungrateful, fickle and deceitful, eager to avoid dangers, and avid for gain, and while you are useful to them they are all with you, offering you their blood, their property, their lives and their sons so long as danger is remote . . . but when it approaches they turn on you.

While men are base creatures and will break a bond of love when it is in their interests, fear underwritten by the threat of punishment will always be effective in securing obedience. If Machiavelli is correct, then it sounds as if people get the governments they deserve.

Though it is useful to be feared, hatred should be avoided. Virtue should not to be the primary aim of a ruler, but neither should wrongdoing. Rather, 'He must stick to the good so long as he can, but being compelled by necessity, he must be ready to take the way of the evil'. As despots from Kim Il Sung of North Korea to Saddam Hussein of Iraq have discovered, once fear has been established it is possible to pretend that your people adore you. Machiavelli would deem this strategy far too risky, although he does counsel deceit as one of a ruler's working methods. A leader should never keep his word when it is disadvantageous to him to do so, but truth must be at least seen to be served. A good ruler will be an expert liar. Similarly, it is a good idea for businesses to seem to be environmentally friendly or sympathetic to their workforces, but it may not be in the financial interests of their shareholders for these to be anything more than pretences. Citizens – or customers or workers – may be reliably wicked, but according to Machiavelli it makes things easier for the ruler if they are also slow-witted, 'For the mob is always impressed by appearances and by results, and the world is composed of the mob.' For one's methods to work, therefore, it may be necessary to keep them hidden. As is often remarked by cynics today, if the people really did appreciate honest politicians they would not keep voting for scoundrels.

At the same time, a ruler should demand that his advisers always tell him the truth. But he should bear in mind that these counsellors are no less wicked and self-interested than the general run of mankind. Punishments, demotions and general bad news should be delivered all at once as circumstances allow, for the less time they are endured the more short-lived will be their after-effects. Favours and good news, on the other hand, should be meted out in small doses over a long period of time so that their effect is longer lasting. Politicians have learned lately to go one better by announcing the same piece of good news, such as increases in public spending, on several different occasions, merely altering the words each time.

A shrewd ruler should be wary of sitting on the fence. According to Machiavelli, decisive action is the best form of prudence. This may come as a surprise to anyone who has found themselves between two warring friends. Supporting one is often a sure way to incur the displeasure of both once they have settled their differences. But even if Machiavelli's advice were to prove useful here, the result would not be a successful friendship, merely a successful power relation. We treat our true friends not as a means to an end – as the ruler treats his consorts – but as ends in themselves. A politician, on the other hand, must be as ready to sacrifice friendship as a friend must be to sacrifice power. In defence of Machiavelli, it might be said that there are no true friendships in politics. In statecraft, he held, you should ally with one or other combatant because, whatever the outcome, you will have placed someone in your debt. A future ruler of Italy – Benito Mussolini – heeded this advice and paid for it with his life. He would have been wiser to follow the path of Spain's dictator Francisco Franco, who offered Hitler only his goodwill and consequently remained in office for thirty-six years until his death at the age of eighty-three. In general, Machiavelli urged that a ruler should lead and defend his weaker neighbours, and strive to weaken the stronger ones. And when the weak argue among themselves, it is better to aid one in crushing the other than risk them both joining against you in the future. Machiavelli was perhaps not cynical enough here, for sometimes intervention leads to that very eventuality.

In 1992, the United States launched Operation Restore Hope to bring aid to war-torn Somalia. The plan swiftly went awry when the Somalis realized that they preferred fighting the Americans to each other. When the US envoy Admiral Howe offered a $25,000 bounty for General Mohamed Aidid, the warlord announced within hours that he would pay $1 million for the capture of 'Animal' Howe. Bill Clinton responded to the rising body-count in textbook Machiavellian style. As his former aide George Stephanopoulos recounted in *All Too Human*, the president declared: 'We're not inflicting pain on these fuckers. When people kill us, they should be killed in greater numbers.' The result was a debacle for the United States, Clinton and all followers of Machiavelli. As the UN spokesman Major Dave Stockwell put it, 'We came, we fed them, they kicked our asses.'

In mitigation, the United States would have faced criticism even if it had left the Somalis to their fate from the beginning. A fickle Western public complains of 'imperialism' when America intervenes and 'heartlessness' when she does not.

Machiavelli, expecting no less from people he regarded as wretches, would be sympathetic:

Let no state think that it can always adopt a safe course; rather should it be understood that all choices involve risks, for the order of things is such that one never escapes danger without incurring another; prudence lies in weighing the disadvantages of each choice and taking the least bad as good.

This is not to say that one's own actions cannot complicate matters. It did not help America's cause that when a meeting of Mogadishu's clan elders was convened on 12 July 1993 to discuss moves towards peace, the house was surrounded by US helicopters and destroyed by missiles, killing over fifty people. Nevertheless, if America should withdraw into isolationism once again and leave the poor and weak of the world to their own devices, no one will be able to say that Machiavelli did not warn them. No prince with any sense will throw good money after bad.

10 | Bacon's Chickens
Predicting the future

Dogs expect to be walked at their regular time and resist changes to their usual route. Humans are no different and go about their daily business in the expectation that what held true yesterday will also hold true tomorrow. The sun will continue to rise in the mornings and objects will fall to the floor rather than floating up to the clouds. We think such events are governed by the laws of nature and can be predicted reliably, but our general expectations are sometimes confounded. Whenever we use a limited number of examples from the past to prove a rule that pertains to *every* example we might see in the future, we are using a method called *induction*. We employ induction when our thoughts move from the particular to the general, or from what we have experienced to what we have not experienced. In the strictest sense, nothing can be truly proved by induction. No matter how many times we have observed something happening in a certain situation, we cannot be absolutely certain that the same thing will happen every time that situation arises. As Bertrand Russell remarked, 'The man who has fed the chicken every day throughout its life at last wrings its neck instead, showing that more refined views as to the uniformity of nature would have been useful to the chicken.' There is no doubt that the fact that something has happened a number of times before causes men and chickens to expect it to happen again. According to Russell, our instincts cause us to believe that the sun will rise again tomorrow, but might we not in fact be in the same position as the doomed fowl? The laws of nature seem to operate as vigorously as ever and have shown no signs of faltering so far, but to argue that nature will be uniform in the future since it always has been in the past is to beg the question. It will, of course, only be uniform in the future if nature is uniform. Given that so much of our everyday life relies on inductive assumptions, it would seem strange to call them irrational, but to many philosophers that is precisely what they are.

The first modern philosopher to give a significant account of induction was Sir Francis Bacon. He was born in London in 1561. As the son of the Lord Keeper of the Great Seal, Sir Nicholas Bacon, Francis was brought up in privilege and educated at Trinity College, Cambridge, Bertrand Russell's twentieth-century alma mater. Bacon's primary career was not in philosophy. He became a lawyer at the age of sixteen and a politician at twenty-three. He was elected to the House of Commons in 1584, where he served for thirty years. From his seat on the benches he issued forth a stream of advice to Elizabeth I on how she should govern the country. This advice was completely ignored, and in 1593 Bacon lost what little influence he had when he opposed a bill for a royal subsidy to pay for further war with Spain.

Bacon got on much better with James I, who ascended to the English throne in 1603 and knighted him in the same year. The king approved of Bacon's views on the royal prerogative and rewarded him with the attorney generalship in 1613. He was made Lord Chancellor and elevated to Baron Verulam in 1618, eventually becoming Viscount St Albans three years later. He conducted his career with the same ethos which he brought to philosophy. Nature, he believed, would give up her secrets gently under close observation and could not be relieved of them by brute force. In affairs of state, he was a schemer who worked by aiming to please those in high places. A notebook has survived in which Bacon assiduously jotted reminders to flatter potential patrons and study the weaknesses of rivals. To the modern sensibility, his worst act was to have taken part in the examination under torture of a clergyman accused of treason. He was, however, loyal to his king, generous with friends and kind to his servants. His indirect approach to power yielded an illustrious career, but his fall, when it came, was precipitous. Barely had he taken his viscount's robes, when he was charged with accepting bribes before the very committee of grievances which he himself headed. Bacon confessed his guilt, but protested that these gifts had not influenced his judgement. In this he was probably telling the truth, as the two plaintiffs complained that their cases had gone against them even though he had accepted their inducements. After a short spell in the Tower of London in 1621, Bacon was banished from Parliament and the court. Although his crime was common among his fellow judges, Bacon magnanimously remarked that the punishment was fit and just. His public life was over, but this did not preclude him from spending the rest of his days writing works of philosophy.

Bacon aimed to restore to man a mastery over nature which he had not enjoyed since the Garden of Eden. The way to go about this, he thought, was not through the abstract speculation of philosophers (which he called 'unfruitful'), but through careful observation of nature and its ways. Bacon argued that the problem with his predecessors' beliefs about nature was that they were either full of dogmatic assumptions or were the result of rash generalization from only a handful of cases. He proposed that general truths should be determined by gradual ascent from smaller to greater degrees of universality. So, since the existence of one black raven cannot prove that all ravens are so coloured, we should begin by checking if all the ravens in, say, the Tower of London are black, then in London, then the rest of the world. Eventually, he hoped, we would arrive at beliefs about the world that applied in all cases and were beyond reasonable doubt. Bacon went about this by compiling tables of his observations and using a process of elimination to find which properties were always present in a given situation and which were merely incidental. Through this method he correctly surmised that heat was caused by the vibration of small particles.

The advantage of Bacon's method is that it is rooted in the world we can see and touch and does not drift off into flights of fancy about the origin of things. But there is a concomitant problem. We would face a tedious task if we took Bacon at his word and began with meagre generalizations before moving on to wider theories. There is so much evidence in the world for so many theories that we would not know where to start, or where to finish. We would also probably die of old age before we had worked through enough observations to arrive at a single law of nature. Unguided observation alone is insufficient. Science also needs hypotheses – reasoned hunches to guide one's research – and these spring from the scientist's imagination and not solely from the world around him. It was not until the nineteenth century and Darwin's research in the Galapagos Islands that science employed Bacon's meticulous, plodding method with unequivocal success.

For all its shortcomings as a means of scientific research, we still rely on induction when we expect sugar to sweeten our coffee rather than make it taste sour. Our belief in this regularity is so ingrained that, should our coffee taste odd one morning, we would assume that we had used salt by mistake rather than think that the sweetening powers of sugar had changed overnight. We do not like to think that such assumptions are rash, for it is not as though the explanations for regularities in the world are total mysteries. When a brick is thrown at a window pane, the pane breaks because glass is brittle and bricks are hard. The breakage does not follow inexplicably from the throw. One event seems to lead to the other 'smoothly' and naturally as we watch it happen. If the brick were to turn into a bunch of flowers upon hitting the window, we would not conclude right away that the throw caused this transformation. We would either think that we have come across a pile of fake bricks that contain hidden flowers or assume that we are hallucinating and should see a doctor. As the sceptic David Hume put it, 'I weigh the one miracle against the other . . . and always reject the greater miracle.' We would only be convinced that throwing a brick does indeed produce flowers if we could watch every step of the process closely to see how it happens, leaving no hidden gaps in which 'magic' could occur. A single observation would be enough to satisfy us if we could see in slow motion the shell of the fake brick crumbling away to reveal the flowers within. We may rely on induction to comprehend the world, but we also derive our expectations from a solid understanding of such things as bricks and flowers.

Sometimes common sense tells us to dismiss conclusions that induction would lead us to believe probable. If the probability of recurrence increases each time something takes place, then the longer we live the more mornings we wake up and therefore the probability of living to see another morning increases with each day of life. By that rationale, I am never less likely to die than on the day I actually do die. We can easily dismiss this conclusion because of our wider understanding of life and death. However, this wider understanding is under-pinned all along by a reliance on induction and the uniformity of nature. I have to observe not just the regularity of my own waking up in the morning, but also the regularity with which individuals of a certain age pass away in their sleep. Thus one induction has been thwarted by a different induction. If we trace the ancestry of understanding far enough, we come to assumptions that rest on a blind faith in the uniformity of nature.

We would be quite mad to distrust this uniformity. It seems that to be a creature of habit is part of what it is to be rational. There are certain principles by which we must live but which we cannot justify by using logic. For example, we believe that jumping from tall buildings is fatal because it has proved so for all those who have tried it. While I cannot prove that it will be just as lethal in the future, I would be thought insane if I put this to the test by throwing myself from a suitable tower. If it is not strictly logical to expect the future to resemble the past, it is certainly no more logical to expect it not to. Bertrand Russell's chicken that has its neck wrung one morning is not a duller creature for expecting to be fed that day. Russell was not alone in underestimating chickens. After conducting an early experiment in refrigeration by stuffing a hen with snow, Sir Francis Bacon contracted a chill and died in 1626.

11 Descartes' Demon
The limits of doubt

The sixteenth-century French essayist Michel de Montaigne remarked: 'It is to place a high value on one's own suppositions to roast others on their account of them.' It has been some time since those in the Western world trusted their beliefs enough to take such measures. The notion that we can never be absolutely certain of anything is the assumption that underpins tolerance. While such doubt enables us to live together socially it can, however, be damaging personally. We have all had the experience of discovering that a firmly held belief is, in fact, false, and then wondering how we can possibly trust our judgement again. If this happens often enough, or to our most important beliefs, the unbridled doubt that ensues can become a serious problem. A betrayal by a lover, for example, can lead us to hold future partners in suspicion too. Most of us continue to live with doubt by degrading the importance of certainty in our world-view. We are content to hold our beliefs merely provisionally, or at least to claim that we do when challenged. Rather than make such a compromise, some philosophers turned instead to attack the power of doubt itself.

The most famous attempt was that of René Descartes, who was born in 1596 in La Haye, France, a small town between Tours and Poitiers which has since been renamed after him. At the age of eight Descartes was sent to the Jesuit college of La Flèche in Anjou, where he studied the philosophy of Aristotle that was dominant at the time, along with the classics and mathematics. A weak and pallid child, Descartes was not expected to live very long. One of the tutors, Father Charlet, took pity on the boy for his frailty and allowed him to lie in every morning – a habit that Descartes was to enjoy for the rest of his life. Far from acquiring a reputation for laziness, his indolence was thought to indicate an early proclivity towards meditation. Descartes himself did nothing to dispel this image and claimed that these mornings spent in bed were the source of his most important philosophical ideas. In 1619, he decided to join the Bavarian army for the opportunities it afforded to see the world. He travelled extensively in Europe as part of his military service though, despite the outbreak of the Thirty Years War in 1618, he does not seem to have participated in any battles. This did not, however, stop him from condemning military life as idle, stupid, immoral and cruel.

In 1628, Descartes settled in Holland, where his more controversial views on philosophy and the natural world would be tolerated (or at least ignored). The Parlement of Paris, by contrast, had passed a decree in 1624 that made attacks on Aristotle punishable by death. Descartes began a work of physics, but hearing that Galileo had been placed under house arrest in 1633 for helping to corroborate Copernicus's heliocentric model of the solar system, he quite reasonably feared a similar fate and did not risk publication. Self-preservation was not his only concern. Throughout his life he wished to gain the respect not only of his peers in philosophy and the sciences, but also of the Catholic Church. A man of religious conviction, he hoped that his work would bolster the faith, but the Church would never be convinced of his piety. In hindsight, the authorities were right to be sceptical. Descartes was part of the new movement of inquiry that led to the Enlightenment and forced religion into retreat. His work in both philosophy and science encouraged the agnostic, while his attempts to construct a rational basis for faith succeeded only in demonstrating the difficulties endemic to such a project. Descartes was as enthusiastic about his prospects for a long life as he was about his work. In 1639 he boasted that he had not been ill for nineteen years and expected to live to be a hundred. Ten years later he accepted a fateful invitation to Stockholm from the nineteen-year-old Queen Christina of Sweden, who thought that instruction from one of the world's greatest thinkers could amuse her in her spare time. She also hoped to make him a Swedish aristocrat with an estate on conquered German land. Descartes immediately regretted his decision. He was a man who enjoyed roaring fires and had developed his most original ideas during a reverie in a stove-heated room. In place of his customary lie-in, he was suddenly expected to brave the elements at five o'clock in the morning – the only time Christina could fit his lessons into her busy schedule. Having complained that the Swedish winter froze men's minds as it froze the water, he contracted a chill one morning in 1650 and died of pneumonia.

Descartes' legacy was the beginning of modern philosophy. With his youthful follies in mind, he wished to elevate our ordinary knowledge about the world to as secure a footing as the eternal truths of geometry and mathematics. Most of us respond to our early errors by changing our opinions, but Descartes undertook to transform the very means by which he formed his views. If so-called philosophical 'certainties' can in fact be doubted, then he decided to suspend belief until he found one that was indubitable. If he could then discern what made such a belief unquestionable, the same method of corroboration could, he hoped, be used to reconstruct the entire edifice of his knowledge. Descartes wrote that his method imitated that of an architect. When an architect wants to build a house on sandy terrain, he starts by digging a set of trenches from which he removes the sand so that he can lay his foundations on firm ground. In the same way, Descartes begins his philosophy by taking everything that is doubtful and throwing it out like sand. In place of a pickaxe, he employs the method of doubt to clear the ground for knowledge.

The demolition begins with the puny human senses from which most of our beliefs are ultimately derived. Our eyesight and hearing sometimes fail us and, as Descartes points out, 'It is prudent never to trust entirely those who have once deceived us.' However, these mistakes are usually made when something is too far away or too small to be properly seen. There are other things which, though derived from the same senses, Descartes plainly could not doubt: for example, that he is sitting by the fire wearing a winter cloak. He could not cast doubt on these facts unless he was a madman, and he declined to take such men as a model for himself. There was still the possibility that he could wake up at any moment to discover that he had not been sitting by the fire at all, but had been asleep and dreaming in his bed. Without the benefit of hindsight, there seems to be no conclusive means by which we can tell if we are awake or dreaming. Most of us have had intensely vivid dreams which we were convinced were real until we awoke. Descartes' response to this problem is to assume that he is indeed dreaming, for there are things about which he cannot be mistaken even if he is asleep. Even our most fantastical visions are not entirely novel. The unicorns that exist only in the imagination are still the product of real things – that is, horns and horses. Admittedly, horns and horses could also be imaginary, but they would still need to be composed of real colours. Moreover, two and three added together make five whether we are awake or asleep. Descartes argues, however, that an omnipotent God might have brought it about that there is no earth or sky, no shape, size, colour or place, but that these things should nevertheless seem to exist. For that matter, God could also have made Descartes commit an error every time he adds two and three together. God presumably has better things to do, but Descartes imagines a malevolent demon, supremely powerful and cunning, who devotes all his energies to deceiving hapless philosophers by placing false images before them and fouling their calculations. This device furnishes Descartes with fully 'hyperbolic' doubt – the fancy that each and every belief he entertains might in fact be false and his every perception illusory.

The easy way out would be to doubt the existence of this demon, but Descartes resolves to stare him down. Assuming he is in the demon's clutches, there is still one thing that he cannot be deceived about: the fact that he, Descartes, exists. In one of the most famous sentences in both philosophy and Latin, he declared, 'Cogito ergo sum: I think, therefore I am.' It is not possible for him to doubt his own existence, for a doubter has to exist in order to doubt.

Unfortunately, Descartes was not so successful in reconstructing knowledge from this foundation. The cogito was true, he maintained, because it was a 'clear and distinct' belief, but his attempts to define what makes an idea clear and distinct are rather vague. Descartes seems to have meant those beliefs that are so clearly correct that they must have been put in front of us by God, and He would not wish to deceive us. For example, we can rest assured that matter always has dimensions and triangles always have three sides. We cannot think of matter without imagining it to have dimensions. Neither can we think of a triangle without imagining it to have three sides. But if God is to underwrite such 'clear and distinct beliefs', we first need to be sure that He exists. Descartes argued that just as the idea of a triangle means that it has three sides, the very idea of God guarantees his existence. This is a variant of the notorious 'ontological argument' – its rationale being that if we imagine God not existing, then we are not imagining God at all but something inferior to Him. For a supposedly perfect being, non-existence is quite an imperfection. It is a matter of clear and distinct apprehension that if we truly imagine an omnipotent, omniscient and immortal being, then we must also imagine him to exist. Ontological arguments fail for a number of reasons, and one is that we do not have to limit them to God. If we were to imagine a perfect human being, for example, existence would presumably have to number among his or her traits, but this does not mean that this perfect individual is therefore walking the earth somewhere.

Even without this problem, Descartes' argument is a circular one, for the veracity of our clear and distinct perceptions rests upon something, namely God, that itself gains credence solely by being a clear and distinct perception.

More can be gained from inspecting the grounds upon which we are able to doubt. Descartes' *cogito* was on the right track, for all doubt must be based on something that is not itself doubted. For example, if I suspect that the 'Picasso' sold to me is a fake, it is because I believe it to be different to the *genuine* works that hang in art collections. Similarly, I can doubt the figure on my restaurant bill because I believe either that I ordered the cheapest item on the menu or that waiters are capable of making mistakes. We need grounds for doubt, and we cannot doubt those grounds at the same time as we use them for doubting other things. Put another way, if we doubt doubts, then we do not doubt at all. Wherever there is scepticism, there must at the same time be something about which we are not sceptical. Reasonable doubt can only ever be partial, and this places severe limits on the demon's ability to deceive us. We can be wrong about certain things, but we cannot be wrong about *everything* – that would deprive us not only of the means to correct our mistakes, but of any basis on which we could say that a mistake was made once the demon has revealed the 'truth'. This demon bewitched Descartes' senses more than he suspected. But instead of persuading him to overestimate what he thought he knew, it led him to underestimate his own abilities as a knowing subject.

In order for the demon to fool us, it must be in possession of a reality that we would recognize and acknowledge once the veil of perception was drawn back. But this requires a body of knowledge we can regard as fixed, in order to make the distinction once we see it. The demon's world envisaged by Descartes is one in which there are no genuine Picassos and neither restaurateurs nor diners ever add up their bills correctly. Even in this scenario there are such things as real fakes and correct bills – it is merely that we do not know them when we see them. That they exist, however, is something we cannot doubt, for otherwise there would be no right answer which our own judgements mistakenly contradict. By denying us the possibility of ever being correct, the demon renders himself and his 'reality' irrelevant.

The true world supposedly hidden from us by the demon is to 'reality' what 'reality' is to our dreams. The demon's victim is in a similar position to the people who claim to have sometimes 'woken up' within a dream and realized their predicament. If I have a dream in which I realize that I am dreaming, this realization too is part of the dream. So how can I tell whether I *really* realized I was dreaming or merely *dreamed* that I did? Let's say that this thought also occurs to me within my dream; it will make no difference, for it is no less a part of my dream than anything else is. My 'realization' cannot be a *true* one, for when I am dreaming, everything that I think, say and do occurs within the context of the dream. My dreaming thoughts cannot penetrate through to the real world in order to be true or false. This inability would be shared by our waking thoughts if every single one of them was the result of the demon's deception. Our thoughts would be unable to actually refer to the real, hidden world of truth known only to our deceiver. They could not be *wrong* about this world because they are not, and can never be, *about* it.

This discussion of the possibility of knowledge might seem subterranean and far removed from ordinary life, but it has very real consequences for our everyday doubts and concerns. A world in which all our lovers could be betraying us, for example, and where we are unable ever to discover this, is not the one in which we live. When our doubts outstrip our capacity to believe the evidence of our senses, we undermine and make ridiculous those very suspicions. We could, of course, be extremely unlucky and take up with a string of adulterous partners. However, the fact that we can discover and recognize betrayal means that we should not give up on fidelity. Every new doubt (in this case, every new dalliance that we accept as truth rather than rumour) in turn becomes grounds for belief. If we trust our powers of detection when they uncover deceit, we should be equally confident in them when they do not.

12 | Hume's Fork
How to skewer nonsense

Character-spotting is a favourite pastime of all who regard themselves as intelligent. Popular myth has it that you can tell someone's 'true character' from the way they dress, how they shake hands, what they laugh at or how they react in a crisis. No matter how innocuous the mannerism, there will be someone who professes to see the course of another's life in it, from the way they light their cigarette to how they fold their handkerchief. The confidence with which these rules are asserted is usually misplaced, and the thought that familiarity with them constitutes the wisdom of age is quite laughable. Those said to 'know people' in this way are merely party to a collection of myths. The prospects for a science of human character are dim not just because – as the philosopher Alasdair MacIntyre noted – our desire to render others predictable is matched by our desire to render ourselves unpredictable to others. According to MacIntyre (1929–), there is a deeper reason why every individual remains an enigma to others, and it is one that impinges upon far more than human behaviour; that is, the fact that *nothing proves anything except itself.* How someone reacts in a crisis reveals only how they react in a crisis; how they fold their handkerchief is emblematic only of how they fold their handkerchief, and nothing more.

This sentiment underpinned the work of the Scottish philosopher David Hume. Hume believed in the ability of science to understand the world, but not if this meant that it would uncover any logically necessary connections between things. We can talk of an apple falling from a tree and grazing the forehead of a sleeper below, but we cannot show that the first event *had* to lead to the other. Necessity, Hume argued, belonged only in the world of mathematics and geometry. When it came to the objects of our senses, all is contingent, and it was bad reasoning to suggest otherwise. We may investigate and record new phenomena, but it is the nature of these phenomena to be self-contained. That is, nothing can be read out of them except for their own nature. They cannot 'point' to truths outside themselves in order to save us the trouble of further experiment and investigation. In the pursuit of knowledge, according to Hume, there are no short cuts.

Hume was born in Edinburgh in 1711. His father, the laird of a very modest estate in the Scottish village of Chirnside, died when David was three years old. Hume and his brother and sister were brought up carefully by their mother Catherine, who ensured that they received a good education. David went to Edinburgh University when he was twelve and studied there for three years. His career began with false starts in commerce and the law. The legal profession, he said, made him feel 'nauseous'. The law's loss was philosophy's gain, though the latter did not realize this straight away. By 1734 Hume was convinced that he could do nothing better with his life than devote it to philosophy. He deported himself to France where he spent three years constructing an entire philosophical system, *A Treatise of Human Nature*. The work was deliberately provocative and its author looked forward to countering the criticisms that he expected to follow publication. However, the *Treatise* 'fell dead-born from the presses' as he put it, and failed to arouse interest let alone controversy. He was to spend much of the rest of his life articulating the same arguments in more appealing garb with much greater success.

Hume's mother once described the young David as a good-natured soul, but a little weak-minded. She was referring to his mental constitution rather than his intelligence, as his early intellectual exertions led him to a nervous breakdown at the age of eighteen. Catherine was right about his gentle nature too, as her son seems to have made no enemies in his personal life save for the paranoid and shameless Jean-Jacques Rousseau (1712–78). Matters were quite different in his professional life, which was dogged by accusations of heresy and atheism. One story tells of an old woman who came across Hume stuck fast up to his waist in deep mud. She finally agreed to haul out the philosopher, but only when he had recited the Apostles' Creed and the Lord's Prayer.

While many clergymen disagreed with Hume's views, they nevertheless became his friends as they found him impossible to dislike. It was his religious opinions, however, that denied Hume the chair of moral philosophy at Edinburgh University in 1744. He left the city in the wake of this disappointment to take up a promising tutorship to an English aristocrat. Unfortunately, the 'Mad' Marquis of Annandale was not only impervious to teaching but also completely insane and Hume extricated himself a year later. In 1746, Hume took a more rewarding post as secretary to General James St Clair, with whom he saw military action in Brittany and travelled on an embassy to Vienna and Turin. From this stint came the splendid scarlet uniform he wears in his most famous portrait and a further position as secretary to the British ambassador to Paris for three years. Literary Paris lavished praise upon the philosopher and he became friends with Rousseau. Hume brought Rousseau back with him to England where the latter's 'enemies' could not reach him. Rousseau's mania later got the better of his gratitude and he repudiated his rescuer, accusing Hume of plotting to kill him. There could have been few less likely assassins than the quiet-tempered Hume, who remained loyal even when betrayed. Perhaps Rousseau was unconventional even in madness and began to judge more, rather than less, by appearances. James Caulfield, the Earl of Charlemont, wrote of Hume:

His face was broad and fat, his mouth wide, and without any other expression than that of imbecility. His eyes vacant and spiritless, and the corpulence of his whole person was far better fitted to communicate the idea of a turtle-eating Alderman, than of a refined philosopher. His speech, in English, was rendered ridiculous by the broadest Scotch accent, and his French was, if possible, still more laughable; so that wisdom, most certainly, never disguised herself before in so uncouth a garb.

Hume eventually returned to Edinburgh. There was not another city in Europe, he remarked, where within a few minutes he could take fifty men of genius and learning by the hand. A gastric affliction which had plagued him for many years entered its final bout in 1776, and he reported: 'I am dying as fast as my enemies, if I have any, could wish, and as easily and cheerfully as my best friends could desire.'

Hume reserved his famous tolerance for his personal affairs. In philosophy he was less accommodating. He had little time for abstract speculation on matters that he deemed unknowable. As Hume would have it, there are but two valid subjects of investigation: relations of ideas and matters of fact. The first concerns geometry and arithmetic. That two multiplied by six is twelve expresses a relation between those numbers that is discoverable by pure thought without recourse to our experience of the world. Likewise, the internal angles of a Euclidean triangle can be proved to add up to 180 degrees without checking one's figures against a triangle drawn on a blackboard. We can regard a mathematical result as certain because to deny it would involve contradicting oneself. Such a truth can be demonstrated without leaving your armchair. The way in which we go about proving matters of fact, on the other hand, is very different. It is possible to assert the contrary of any matter of contingent fact without contradicting oneself. The possibility that the sun might not rise tomorrow is every bit as conceivable as its rising in the normal fashion. To settle the matter, it is necessary to go out into the world and consult our experience. For matters that can be settled neither by mathematical reasoning nor empirical observation, Hume suggests a simple verdict. Known as 'Hume's Fork', it proceeds:

When we run over libraries, persuaded of these principles, what havoc must we make? If we take in our hand any volume; of divinity or school metaphysics, for instance; let us ask, Does it contain any abstract reasoning concerning quantity or number? No. Does it contain any experimental reasoning concerning matter of fact and existence? No. Commit it then to the flames: for it can contain nothing but sophistry and illusion.

Hume would throw quite a few of our common-sense inferences on to the bonfire; among them our beliefs that there is a self at the heart of a person, that there are observable laws of nature and that there is a mechanism of cause and effect in the world. These are things to which we ascribe necessity – we think that perceptions demand a perceiver, that regularities demand laws and that consequences demand causes. Hume would argue that we inject an unwarranted element into their description. We have perceptions, but we do not see them being *perceived*. We observe regularities in nature, but we do not observe *laws of nature*. We see one event following another, but we do not see an event *causing* another, that is, necessitating it. For that matter, we move our arms to hail taxis, but we do not observe the operation of our will on our arms. We may intend to wave at a passing cab, but this intention does not cause our arms to move, for we might change our mind at the last moment. After that last moment, we do not intend to raise our arm at all – we just raise it. Yet we are wont to take a number of facts and infer a further fact from them. We see a cue ball striking a red which then shoots into the pocket and we think that the first event caused the second. By caused, we mean that the consequence had to follow by necessity. This necessity is not itself something we observe, however. We see the first ball striking the second, and then the latter moving to the pocket, but that is all we see – so the necessity cannot be an ordinary fact of the kind we can observe directly. The necessity cannot be a relation of ideas either, because it is conceivable that the second ball should have stopped where it was and sent the cue ball backwards, for instance. We could infer the consequence if we wished, but it would only be on the basis of what usually happens in a game of snooker or pool. Our belief in the necessity at hand does not rely on reasons at all, Hume concludes; it is simply a habit we have acquired through frequently observing one event to follow another.

Our experiences of cue balls explain our expectations, but strictly speaking they do not justify them. Habits are not the kind of thing that can be justified. They can become more ingrained, but they do not become better supported each time the expectations they deliver are fulfilled. Experience, Hume continues, only shows us how one event constantly follows another. It does not show us any secret link which makes the two inseparable. If it did somehow show such a link, then the link would become a new fact – it would be as inert as the first two events and would stand in need of another hidden connection to link it to the others. We might, for example, look closely at what happens when the cue ball collides with the red and see the latter's surface contract and expand again, propelling it away, but now we have only uncovered a new event and not a necessary connection of any kind. If we could witness the cue ball's movement *causing* the red's, that would mean it would be inconceivable for the second event not to happen – and this is not the case (as it never is with events in the world).

It is possible to ascribe necessity to mathematical truths because they do not tell us anything substantial about the way things are in the world. Two times six, for example, still equals twelve even if objects never in fact occur in dozens. Mathematics can deal in necessity because its answers are guaranteed by the meaning of its questions. In the same way, bachelors are necessarily single men and wives are necessarily married. The statement 'All bachelors are single men' is necessarily true because it is a tautology, and anyone who denied it would simply be misunderstanding the words in the sentence. Hume's thought is that mathematical truths are also dressed-up tautologies. Unfortunately, tautologies are of little use in judging the character of strangers or predicting the outcome of football matches.

None of this means that our firm expectations about the course of the world cannot turn out to be correct – indeed, they usually are correct or we would not have them in the first place. It does mean, however, that the foundation of our expectations is found in habit rather than reason.

13 | Reid's Common Sense
The philosophy of the obvious

Common sense is not something for which philosophers are famous. Bertrand Russell once remarked that the point of philosophy is a matter of starting with something so simple as to seem not worth stating, and ending with something so paradoxical that no one will believe it. A cynic would say that stating the obvious is unlikely to get a thinker into the history books. Some philosophers, however, have bucked this tradition and argued that the instincts we find useful in ordinary life are also the best ones with which to tackle the great questions of existence. They deserve their place in history because their reasons for supporting the obvious are anything but banal.

The original champion of common-sense reasoning was the Scottish philosopher Thomas Reid, born in Kincardine in 1710. Reid's illustrious family included his brother, Alexander, who was physician to King Charles I, and his great-uncle, James Gregory, who invented the reflecting telescope. Thomas came from a long line of Presbyterian church ministers and entered the family profession after studying philosophy at Marischal College, Aberdeen. As a preacher he did not electrify his congregation, but he did win their respect and admiration through his level-headedness and decency. The historian of Scottish philosophy James McCosh wrote of Reid in 1875: 'He is in every respect, a Scotchman of the genuine type: shrewd, cautious, outwardly calm, and yet with a deep well of feeling within, and capable of enthusiasm; not witty, but with a quiet vein of humour.' This 'well of feeling' was in evidence every time Reid administered the Sacrament in his church, and he would frequently shed tears when he referred to the love of

Christ. In addition to his religious duties, Reid felt obligated to defend the philosophical instincts of the common man, or 'the vulgar' as he put it. He was horrified upon reading the sceptical philosophy of his countryman David Hume. According to Hume, we could not be certain that one event ever causes another, that the laws of nature will continue in the same way, or even that there is such a thing as an external world independent of our sense impressions. In 1752, Reid took up a professorship of philosophy at King's College, Aberdeen, and set about the project of restoring the common-sense beliefs that Hume had demolished.

In Aberdeen, and later at Glasgow University, Reid's unobvious talent for teaching eventually gave rise to the common-sense school of philosophy. One of his pupils wrote:

In his elocution and mode of instruction there was nothing peculiarly attractive. He seldom, if ever, indulged himself in the warmth of extempore discourse; nor was his manner of reading calculated to increase the effect of what he had committed to writing. Such, however, was the simplicity and perspicuity of his style, such the gravity and authority of his character, and such the general interest of his young hearers in the doctrines which he taught, that, by the numerous audiences to which his instructions were addressed, he was heard, uniformly, with the most silent and respectful attention.

Reid often asked his pupils to appeal to their instincts when discussing truth. Common-sense beliefs, he maintained, are the ones we cannot help holding because of our nature as human beings (or, in today's terms, those we are 'hard-wired' to accept). Though individuals can contradict their intuitions, he admitted, they cannot do so without suffering psychological upheaval. This may well be true to a large degree, but it does not mean that beliefs which cause mental strife are not correct. Some individuals considered mad in their day (and who sometimes were indeed mad – such as the philosopher Friedrich

Nietzsche) have later been acknowledged as great geniuses. Hume himself suffered a kind of nervous breakdown while formulating his arguments for scepticism. In defence of Reid's point, however, it seems intuitively plausible that beliefs leading to nervous breakdowns are less likely to be true than ones which leave us sane. The human race would not have survived if our instincts were hopelessly idiotic. In the main, they lead us to act sensibly: jumping off cliffs, into snake pits or on to bonfires are all strongly discouraged by common sense. A tendency towards philosophical scepticism, on the other hand, would not have stood our ancestors in good stead if, rather than fleeing at the sight of a hungry lion, they paused to question the beast's objective existence.

Reid would have regarded our behaviour around lions as a good example of inbuilt common sense, which he believed could often be divined by looking at what is consistent in all peoples. Unfortunately, notions that are deemed 'common-sensical' in one place may not be given this distinction in another. Such beliefs are often informed less by human nature than by the particular mores and notions of a given culture at a given time. To the Fang tribesmen of pre-modern Equatorial Guinea, nothing was more commonsensical than the idea of acquiring your enemies' spirit and strength through eating them for dinner.

What constitutes common sense can change over time. Ethics textbooks for philosophy students in the early twentieth century often began with a chapter on the 'common-sense' view that moral values were objective facts. Contemporary volumes still begin with the common-sense view, only this view is now that ethics are a matter of subjective opinion. The only way to tell whether a belief really is part of human nature is to see whether it has seemed obvious to all peoples in all eras. And even then people may feel differently in the future. At one time or another, common sense has assured us that insects grow out of dirt particles, that the human body could not withstand travelling at the speeds attainable by steam engines and that the world is a flat disc that lies at the centre of the universe. Reid assumed, furthermore, that two beliefs dictated by common sense can never conflict with one another, but things are not always so simple. Those who campaign for lower taxes on the basis of 'common-sense' economics are sometimes the same people who argue the case for better-funded public transport because it too contributes to wealth creation. Since it was the cause of their dilemma, common sense itself can suggest no means of settling it for them.

Meanwhile, humanity has made great strides by embracing ideas that fly in the face of our natural instincts, such as quantum theory or the notions that the earth is round rather than flat and orbits the sun rather than vice versa. While common sense seems fairly effective when it comes to self-preservation, it is not so reliable in the realm of more abstruse matters of fact. For example, the physicist Erwin Schrödinger (1887–1961) imagined a box in which there is a cat and a mechanism for releasing cyanide gas controlled by the radioactive decay of an atom. According to quantum theory, whether or not the atom decays and sets off the poison is entirely random and cannot be predicted. The fact is undetermined until we actually open the box and inspect the mechanism. This means, however, that until we do so the unfortunate feline is neither alive nor dead but in some indeterminate live-dead state. Human minds find this difficult to accept at present, but to our descendants it may seem no more troublesome than the fact that the earth is spherical.

Reid argued further that what are supposedly mere instincts are not necessarily inferior to the dictates of reason. He explained his position thus:

The sceptic asks me, Why do you believe the existence of the external object which you perceive? This belief, sir, is none of my manufacture; it came from the mint of Nature; it bears her image and superscription; and, if it is not right, the fault is not mine: I even took it upon trust, and without suspicion. Reason, says the sceptic, is the only judge of truth, and you ought to throw off every opinion and every belief that is not grounded on reason. Why, sir, should I believe the faculty of reason more than that of perception? – they came both out of the same shop, and were made by the same artist; and if he puts one piece of false ware into my hands, what should hinder him from putting another?

It was in this vein that Reid attacked the Lockean doctrine of ideas upon which Hume's scepticism was partly based. John Locke (1632–1704) and his successors in the empiricist tradition argued that we never perceive objects directly in the external world, but only our ideas or impressions of them. So, in effect, perception is the mental apprehension of mental objects. Since everything to do with cognition goes on in the mental sphere, then either we can never tell whether our ideas correspond with physical objects or, if we can, it is because objects themselves must be ideas too, as the idealist George Berkeley (1685–1753) argued. Reid realized that this merely replaces one problem with another of equal size. Locke had begun with the question of how our mental states connect with objects in the world, but he solved it only by creating a new problem of how our mental states connect with objects in the mind. Now that we have the history of philosophy at our disposal, we can see that the way in which this second problem was framed and tackled makes it suspiciously similar to the first. According to Reid, however, the second problem puts us in an even more mystified position. Locke's theory could only help our understanding if the ideas he introduces as the new objects of perception are less obscure than the old ones – that is, ordinary physical objects.

One does not have to read Locke's often demanding works to guess that this is not the case. It is simpler, and certainly more faithful to common sense, to assume that we have perceptions, however unreliable, of physical objects rather than perceptions of ideas which in turn may or may not be related to those objects. As William of Ockham would say, to bring mental objects into the equation would be to multiply entities beyond necessity. Neither does introducing mental objects place our knowledge on surer ground, for Locke has created the zero-sum game that leads to scepticism: the more sure we are about the objects of knowledge, the less sure we can be about the significance of that knowledge. In other words, though we can be certain that we perceive our ideas, we still cannot be certain that those ideas have any correspondence whatsoever with the world. And if this theory has no better grounding than the alternative dictated by common sense, as far as Reid was concerned our decision between instinct and skepticism is easy.

The strength of Reid's argument lies less in supporting the claims of received ideas than in placing the burden of proof on those who would refute them. As an old philosopher's saying goes, 'Every conclusion is the disproof of its premises.' The more absurd our conclusions, the more doubt this casts on the grounds from which we derived them – even if those grounds seemed reasonable and uncontroversial before we began to reason from them. If our common-sense beliefs are the ones we feel most sure about, then they will be doubly difficult to shift because they are more convincing than the grounds of any argument that leads us to question them. We do not need, therefore, to justify our belief in the external world – to Reid, what stands in need of strong justification is the ludicrous-sounding notion that reality might be an illusion. This point was taken up by the English philosopher G. E. Moore in the early twentieth century. Moore (1873–1958) famously pointed out that a sceptical argument claiming that he had no hands could never be as convincing as the evidence of his own two hands held up in front of his face.

If nothing else, Reid's warnings remind us that if we wish to depart from common sense in our beliefs, we had better be sure that we are getting something worth while from this betrayal of our instincts. Four centuries earlier, William of Ockham advised us only to complicate matters if by doing so we can explain things better than if we keep things simple. Similarly, Reid proposes that we should dismiss common sense only if the alternative is clearly more compelling than what our first instincts lead us to believe. Common-sense beliefs must always be taken seriously, if only because one will not get very far in persuading anyone against them otherwise. If there is an existing theory, perhaps long-held, that seems to explain our experiences adequately, then we are rightly wary of claims against it. If we find our beliefs overturned all too quickly and easily, we may start to become suspicious. This is because, while evidence for a counterintuitive view is being amassed, a wholly different question arises: if the new theory is so succinct, so well-supported and so clearly correct, then how on earth could we have been so dim as to hold our former beliefs, let alone regard them as commonsensical? One might say that the stronger the case for a controversial new theory, the stronger the explanation must be for why we ever believed the contrary.

Take, for example, the new orthodoxy that drinking alcohol is good for you. The healthcare organization Bandolier takes the results of medical trials conducted around the world and amalgamates them to attain the largest possible test base. In January 2000 it published a ten-point summary of advice on healthy living based on its research. This was number five on its list:

Drink alcohol regularly. The type of alcohol probably doesn't matter too much, but the equivalent of a couple of glasses of wine a day or a couple of beers is a good thing. The odd day without alcohol won't hurt either. Think of it as medicine.

For years we had been taught to think of alcohol as poison. This intuitive view was confirmed every time an alcoholic developed cirrhosis of the liver, not to mention every time we suffered a hangover. Even a single shot of vodka, doctors told us, can destroy thousands of brain cells. Those who now encourage moderate drinking do not seek to deny this, however, and they would have been ridiculed by the medical profession if they had denied the deleterious effects of mammoth drinking sessions. Instead they claim that alcohol is still good for you even though the basis for our common-sense view of the demon drink is correct. If they did not agree with the rest of us on the harmful effects of excessive consumption, we would see no reason to believe their view of the benefits of smaller quantities. Drinking two bottles of vodka can still kill you; it is just that it is more like taking an overdose of paracetamol than an overdose of arsenic. We are also given a plausible account of why the positive effects of drinking previously went unnoticed: it is because they are recognizable only from a sizeable study of various cases backed up by biochemical research – a means not available to the individual who is using only his or her common sense.

It was necessary, for argument's sake, for researchers to show that the old view of drinking was a reasonable one on the strength of the best evidence available. Such an account actually adds nothing to the validity of an argument against a common-sense view, but what it does add is plausibility – and this was the very quality on which Thomas Reid thought our instincts could not be bettered. Perhaps in the future we will discover that many of the beliefs we regard as unassailable are in fact mistaken, but should someone propose that heroin addiction is psychologically beneficial, or that a stable marriage is no environment in which to bring up children, the onus of proof must fall upon these revolutionaries rather than on the traditionalists.

Rousseau's Contract
Learning from fiction and fantasy

The world around us does not always cooperate with philosophy in the task of making it easier to think clearly. When we look for the basis of values and institutions, we sometimes find nothing at all. Our creations may in reality be arbitrary and, to an extent, irrational. In an English courtroom, men and women sit around in wigs and gowns invoking the powers of 'law' and the 'commonwealth' to justify depriving miscreants of their liberty. Despite all the talk of sacred laws and texts, what is actually going on is one group of individuals pitting a judgement against another, and then exerting the physical force of the prison service to effect a punishment – even if the accused deserves this treatment. But the legal system would be undermined if this was made explicit, hence the wigs and gowns and the language of 'justice'. 'By the powers invested in him', the taxman takes away a portion of your earnings and gives them, in England at least, to 'Her Majesty's Government'. Since you have no choice in the matter, there is little essential difference between a world in which your income is dispatched on official forms bearing the seals of state and one in which a group of men with cudgels arrive at your house to demand payment. It would be less efficient, and would certainly look less civilized, however, if taxes were collected in this way. If we are to stay sane and maintain that our institutions serve us well, we have to act *as if* the basis was quite different – as if, perhaps, our values and institutions came from the will of God or the dictates of Natural Law.

There is certainly something to be said for staring the truth down in this way. Life would scarcely be possible otherwise.

This does not mean that the real facts of the matter are to be swept under the carpet in embarrassment. We can admit that our actions are in accordance with a pure fiction without suggesting that all fictions are as good as each other. Physicists work on the model that quarks and electrons are elementary particles, but this does not stop them from trying to discover even more basic constituents of matter. Though their theories of quarks and electrons are provisional, they are also the product of long and difficult work and explain more about the universe than was possible before. In fact, the historical development of our most important fictions has been every bit as hard-fought as the search for truth. The French philosopher Jean-Jacques Rousseau, for example, helped formulate the doctrine of the 'social contract' that binds the rights and duties of citizens and governments. Under this system, the individual gives up certain freedoms – such as the right to take home all of his earnings – in order to obtain other benefits from the state, such as the protection of his property by a police force. The social contract cannot be found in any museum or library and no one can remember signing it, but the very idea of it none the less underpins what we expect from our government and what that government expects from us.

Born in 1712 in Geneva, Jean-Jacques Rousseau became one of the most influential thinkers of the Enlightenment. His mother died in childbirth and he was raised by his father, a watchmaker who greatly enjoyed the status he had acquired by marrying into the upper classes. A cruel and dissolute man, Rousseau senior provided no tutelage for his son and apparently showed him little affection. As a writer, Rousseau was to campaign for the loving care of children, but his own progeny received even worse treatment than their grandfather meted out. When Rousseau was ten, his father drew his sword during a brawl and was forced to flee Geneva upon threat of imprisonment. His son was deposited with his mother's less-than-welcoming family, who over the next six years completed his education in contempt. At the age of sixteen, Rousseau ran away to earn a living working for wealthy families in Italy. After the death of one employer, he was accused of stealing from her house. He blamed the offence on a maid, who was then duly punished for the crime. He seems to have felt little guilt as a consequence and later explained that he had felt such affection for the girl that when he was questioned she had been the first person to enter his head. Thus absolved, he posed as a Roman Catholic convert in Savoy and found a benefactress in Madame de Warens. He became her secretary and lover and, though he claimed to abhor her morals, he found her a useful teacher of the self-serving arts. She was also a highly cultured woman and during his eight years in her company Rousseau acquired much of the learning in philosophy, literature and musicianship that he had lacked. By the time Madame de Warens tired of him, he was ready to make his fortune among the young radicals of Paris.

Soon after his arrival in 1741, Rousseau met Thérèse Le Vasseur, a plain and illiterate laundry maid. They began a long affair that produced five children – all of whom Rousseau abandoned to an orphanage. He still had the nerve to claim: 'I know full well no father is as tender as I would have been.' A friend of the painter Delacroix once saw Rousseau walking in the Tuileries when a child accidentally kicked a ball into the philosopher's leg. The self-styled defender of innocents flew into a rage and pursued the child with his cane. Despite his flawed character, Rousseau achieved musical success with his operas and an opening into the world of letters after he made friends with Denis Diderot and the other *philosophes* of the *Encyclopédie* in the early 1740s. He soon became the foremost of these iconoclasts, the most vigorous in conversation and the most talented in prose.

Rousseau's early political ideas took shape when he had an 'illumination' while on the way to visit Diderot (1713–84) in Vincennes (the latter was in prison there for his attacks on established religion). The thought came to him that modern progress, instead of exalting man, had corrupted him. We were not the fallen creatures of Catholic doctrine, but quite the reverse. In the 'state of nature' prior to civilization, Rousseau contended, we were 'noble savages', happy and good. Since that time, unhappiness had come to prevail via the 'artificial' constraints imposed on our liberty by society. Far from increasing our freedom, the arts and sciences had merely strengthened the oppressive powers of the state. To the English philosopher Thomas Hobbes (1588–1679), life in the state of nature had been 'solitary, poor, nasty, brutish and short'. Rousseau agreed that it was solitary, but argued that it was when we started to live together that all the trouble began. The bonds of affection that developed when men and women shared homes also heralded jealousy and resentment. This was compounded by the 'civilized' notion of private property which, in seeking to protect individuals' belongings, artificially sanctified material inequalities between the rich and the poor. Even the rich are not happy, for their materialist values mean that they will never be satisfied with what they have. Thus we exchanged our natural rights for bogus civic ones under the terms of a fraudulent social contract.

In his 1762 masterpiece *The Social Contract*, Rousseau called for a redrafting of this agreement. 'Man was born free, but he is everywhere in chains,' he began. In a better society, he argued, men would not submit cravenly to the law, but would readily give up the right to act as they please in exchange for true liberty. This true liberty would consist of acting in accordance with laws imposed by the people on themselves rather than as dictated by the powerful. This would not be the will of an individual, as the will of one man or woman can conflict with that of another, but rather the *general* will that people express as a society. The general will is to further the interest of the many rather than to serve the few, and occasionally it may not coincide with the will of a particular individual. The rights we forgo in our involvement should not be lamented, however, because unbridled freedom effectively leads to the rule of the strongest – which is exactly what Rousseau wished to abolish by tearing up the original social contract. Though the social contract of the new republic would be artificial and no less a fiction than its predecessor, it would be legitimated by the consent of its 'signatories' and its contribution to the general happiness. Any government that did not guarantee such liberty would have broken the agreement and abrogated its right to rule. This idea was pertinent to both the American and French Revolutions. The United States' Declaration of Independence in 1776 resembles a legal contract drawn up between two parties – in this case citizens and rulers. Moreover, an individual who 'refused' to sign the contract by breaking the law was wilfully giving vent to his passions and not acting rationally: only punishment would make him aware of what he really wanted. Punishment under the contract is a way of 'forcing people to be free'. Thus the social contract is a fiction, but it is based on the truth of our desires.

However, for Rousseau, the fiction of the social contract did not stop there, as he believed that the general will was fallible. In his view, most people are fools and need a wise leader to direct them towards their true interests. Therein lies the rub, for we now have a volte-face in Rousseau's thought whereby if we cannot give ourselves wholly to nature, we must give ourselves wholly to the state. For the purposes of efficiency and in order to exploit the citizens' obedience to their 'true' nature, he continued, it might even be for the best if their leader claimed divine sanction. Needless to say, the history of such systems is a dark one, but Rousseau was trying to find a realistic means of making the human lot a better one rather than preaching a utopia. In his own mind at least, he was concerned with useful fictions, not fantasies. Nowadays, of course, something similar to divine sanction is claimed by our rulers even though most of us are no fools. Politicians are fond of saying that they are the servants of the people, whose will they are mandated to execute through the instruments of democracy. They sometimes persist in this charade even when public opinion is clearly against them, but come election time, the electorate has the chance to judge whether or not their leaders have broken their contract.

After attacks of paranoia led Rousseau to distrust everyone but Thérèse, the two married in 1768. Rousseau claimed he had never loved Thérèse but, with the many contradictions in his life and thought, this cannot be taken too seriously. Rousseau was a hypocrite, but if hypocrisy disbarred one from teaching then nothing would ever get taught. Though his egalitarian ethical views – whereby the individual should 'alienate himself, with all his rights, to the whole of the community' – helped lead to the totalitarian horrors of Nazism and Stalinism, the quasi-legal status of the social contract also informed the constitutions of the democracies to come. The dangers inherent in Rousseau's ideas were realized when we began to take his fiction literally. If the social contract had remained an imaginary and convenient means to an end (that of ensuring liberty), much suffering could have been avoided. Too many revolutionaries, however, thought of the social contract as an end in itself – believing, perhaps, that people did indeed desire to subjugate themselves completely to authority. The social contract was such a powerful idea that they could not help themselves. The answer is not merely to keep a closer eye on reality, but also to treat our fictions with the respect they deserve *as fictions* – and to appreciate what they do for us without demanding that which was never promised.

15 | Kant's Spectacles
Putting man at the centre of the universe

Hi-fi buffs can detect differences in the clarity of musical recordings that a non-enthusiast would never notice. They devote large amounts of time and money to acquiring amplifiers and speaker systems that produce a sound as faithful as possible to the original performance. But even the most advanced hi-fi system falls short of perfection. At some point in the process from the recording to the playback, impurities creep in that keep the next generation of electronics firms in business. There may come a time, however, when audio technology is so sophisticated that the only limitations an enthusiast will have to suffer are not those of his stereo system, but of the human ear itself. At this point, philosophers will have something to say about hi-fis. Whatever the ear adds or subtracts from a crystal-clear recording will not be a difference in quality, but in kind. We hear sounds the way we do because of the particular structure our ears have. A creature with a different kind of ear – a bat, for example – might hear things quite differently because its auditory system works on a different range of frequencies to our own. Ear canals with different structures affect how things sound to their possessors – just as different kinds of cameras take different kinds of photographs. When we describe a tune we have heard, we are describing not only the sound itself, but also something about the way human ears work. We cannot help doing this, as we have no way of listening other than the one we have. Since the same goes for all our senses, the way we understand the world is partly tied to the faculties we use to arrive at that understanding.

Our perceptions are not purely passive – we do not simply

sit and drink them in. Whenever we taste a flavour or hear a sound we are also actively *doing* something. It is just that our brains are so used to ordering and processing the world that we do not notice them doing it. To perceive the world is to change it. This was the central insight of the German philosopher Immanuel Kant. The seventeenth-century English philosopher John Locke famously declared that the human mind was born *tabula rasa* – a blank slate upon which the world leaves its imprints as we learn and grow older. This thought led to the sceptical philosophy of Hume's Fork, under which the knowledge that we possess innately is trivial and self-referential while significant knowledge can be discovered only through experience and observation. The search for substantial knowledge that could be attained purely through thought was not yet over. Kant was the first philosopher to suspect that there might be some residual innate knowledge hidden from even Hume's gaze.

Kant was born in Königsberg in East Prussia in 1724. His father was a saddler from what Kant claimed was Scottish immigrant stock, while his mother was an uneducated but highly intelligent German woman. The family faith was the dour Lutheran pietism which prescribed the simple life under the observance of the moral law. Kant became a student of theology at the University of Königsberg in 1740 and began his first book, a work on physics, at the age of twenty. When he failed to secure an academic post six years later he was forced to work as a tutor for affluent families. This period lasted for fifteen years but was not an unhappy one. It introduced Kant to city society and provided opportunities for (by his own standards) exotic travel. His most distant excursion was to the town of Arnsdorf sixty miles away – further from his birthplace than he would ever journey again. It was wide reading rather than travel that broadened Kant's mind. Though he was weakened by a deformed chest and stood only five feet tall, he proved a sensation in the lecture room. A naturally engaging speaker, he enriched his talks with jokes and literary references and lectured on every subject from Newtonian physics to land-forms and fireworks to great public acclaim. He was offered the professorship of poetry at Berlin University but declined the position in favour of the sedentary hometown life he had come to prefer. His peace and quiet were already interrupted by the droves of young philosophers and government officials who came to Königsberg to absorb his wisdom. Even so he still managed to maintain his daily regime of constitutional walks, such that people were able to set their clocks by his appearance in the streets. His favourite street was renamed 'The Philosopher's Walk' after him. Only once was his absence noted, and he explained that he had found Rousseau's *Émile* so absorbing that he had to stay at home to finish it.

In 1755, Kant returned to the University of Königsberg to complete his degree. He began teaching there the following year, spurred into creative work by reading the philosophy of David Hume, which he said woke him from his 'dogmatic slumbers'. In 1781, Kant emerged with a new philosophy that he called 'transcendental criticism'. As with so many philosophers, controversial religious beliefs got him into trouble. After the publication of *Religion Within the Boundaries of Pure Reason* in 1793 – a work expressing views which questioned traditional Christian doctrine – King Frederick William II ordered him to stop writing and teaching on religious matters. Kant obeyed his orders to the letter, at least until the king's death. But he was an old man by this time and his health was failing, and soon afterwards he retired to re-edit his works. He died in 1804. Inscribed on his tomb are the words: 'The starry heavens above me and the moral law within me' – the two things that he wrote 'fill the mind with ever new and increasing admiration and awe, the oftener and the more steadily we reflect on them'.

Kant wished to strike a new path between the two strands of eighteenth-century philosophy. The rationalists had argued that reason can comprehend the world unaided by the senses, whereas the empiricists maintained that all knowledge must be firmly grounded in experience. Both have their weaknesses – knowledge secured through pure reason may be indubitably true but says little about the way the world is. Empirical knowledge can say much about the world, on the other hand, but sacrifices certainty in payment. Kant's efforts achieved nothing short of a revolution in philosophy. Where philosophers had previously talked either of objects or our perceptions of them, Kant realized that the means by which the two meet is especially important. Metaphysics – the attempt to philosophize the nature of reality – had proceeded, Kant maintained, in entirely the wrong way, and this is what left it open to Hume's attack. Hume had argued that knowledge of the sensible world would never be attained through means other than the senses. Since Plato, the alternative suggested by philosophers was that thought could apprehend parts of reality that the senses could never reach, such as souls, the nature of God and the universe as a whole.

Kant dismissed this sort of thinking as 'mystical' and introduced a new metaphysics in its place. The fact remains that we perceive objects through the senses, he argued, but we would be mistaken in thinking that our eyes and ears deliver them as they truly are. Everything that we perceive, and thenceforth understand, is processed by the senses upon arrival. Their mediation imposes a character upon our experiences that is not itself part of the objects we are perceiving. Every object that we perceive is given to us at a certain point in space and time, but we do learn of space and time through experience because we never perceive objects that are not in space and time. With mundane objects such as apples, we might reach the general concept of 'apple' from seeing several Granny Smiths and Coxes. The concept of space, on the other hand, is not something we abstract from instances of it in the world because everything from which space might be abstracted already presupposes it. Unless we already understood space, and thought in terms of space, we would not be able to talk of anything as being 'in a certain place' or 'above' or 'below' something else. Even if I can imagine space without anything in it, I am unable to imagine anything in it without also imagining space. Such 'forms' of our experience must be built into our intuition and known to us before we open our eyes for the first time. It is as if we are wearing space-and-time tinted spectacles that we can never take off.

Kant held that there are several ways – twelve to be precise – in which the mind orders experience. The most important one is the assumption of cause and effect, according to which everything that happens is the result of a preceding event that determines its character. In Kant's view, it is the attempt to apply these general forms to objects beyond our experience that leads to the futility of traditional metaphysics. One example is the mistaken 'proof' of God's existence that identifies him as the prime mover – the cause that does not itself have a cause but to which all events can ultimately be traced. The existence of a prime mover can never be proved, but it is equally futile to attempt to disprove it. Better to be done with all such speculation and give up the hope of knowing transcendent truths. Where Plato would have us innately knowing objects (even if it is very difficult to retrieve them from the back of one's mind), Kant has us innately knowing the general form which reality will take. Empiricists claimed that any innate knowledge must be trivial or tautologous, but the kind that Kant ascribes to us is neither, because human beings might have possessed different means of processing their experiences. The nature of our eyes and ears is as contingent as the world they are used to perceive.

A further consequence of Kant's view is that the true nature of objects remains unknowable. Our knowledge may hint at things-in-themselves, or 'noumena' as Kant calls them, but the innate character of anything cannot be discerned. When we look upon a garden, for example, we do not see it as it really is but receive an impression that our eyes have filtered and made suitable for our delectation. A worker bee might see a very different vista – as its eyes can detect ultraviolet light – but this insect too would be ignorant of the garden as it is in-itself. The mediation of our faculties means that we never apprehend objects as they are in-themselves, prior to being perceived, but only a humanized version of them. Owning processing faculties makes knowledge possible, but all faculties come with this limit attached. Human knowledge has no Garden of Eden in which unalloyed truths can be known. But this does not mean that our ability to understand the world has fallen from grace, merely that all knowledge is coloured by mediation. Any other system of perception would face similar limits.

One response to these arguments is to cast aside any notion of an understanding that cuts through bias and prejudice to see the world 'as it really is'. Kant, however, did not go this far. He held that there are different grades of purity within our understanding of the world. For example, he argued that a proper apprehension of aesthetic beauty is one that is limited to an appreciation of an object's pure form – that is, one that is not tainted by any interest other than the purely aesthetic. This yields the odd conclusion that a man is not thinking primarily of a woman's beauty when he finds her sexually attractive. A morally virtuous act, meanwhile, is one that is done out of pure, cold duty rather than a feeling that it is rather nice to help old ladies across the road. Kant's preference for 'pure' motives is not made on moral grounds, however. Instead, he determines what constitutes moral behaviour by reference to what is most pure in the faculties of human beings: rationality. In our relations with one another, this means obedience to universal duties that are untarnished by personal preferences. However, to apply Ockham's Razor and make the minimum claim suggests that one method is more purely rational than the other rather than more moral.

Kant sets extremely high standards when he accuses human perception of being inherently biased. It is wrong, he argues, to hope that we can observe the world as it really, truly is, unsullied by human categories, but then it would be better not to think of it as being 'sullied' by us. This is not the language Kant uses, but it is what his account implies. Kant is often tempted to view things-in-themselves not simply as things-in-themselves, but as shining and highly desirable jewels of pure truth. There is consequently a tension in his work between the purity we can never attain and the attempt to edge ever closer to that purity. He was perhaps betraying his first principles by indulging in a detailed account of the mediation between our senses and the world. It is questionable whether our mediating faculties are not also things-in-themselves which must remain forever out of reach. In Kant's favour, the fact that our knowledge will always be coloured by the kind of creatures we are is no excuse for taking things as they come and accepting them at face value. For example, when most of us listen to a new pop single and judge it good or bad, our verdict is influenced by the context in which we hear it, the image of the band and their previous output in addition to the quality of the song itself. We gain a clearer view by listening to it in different surroundings – since some songs are better suited to night-clubs than sitting rooms, for instance – and by disregarding the haircuts, clothes and opinions of the performers. We can never attain a perfectly objective view – because the song has to be heard in *some* context – but varying the setting can be instructive. Also, as in the case of punk and heavy metal, the accoutrements of the music may be just as important as the tunes themselves. Listening to such bands with an ear only for harmony defeats the object somewhat. When it comes to such questions of taste, Kant's essential point is as relevant as ever: pure knowledge is merely pure *human* knowledge, and the study of our faculties is at least as valid an inquiry into the nature of things as a straightforward study of the world itself.

16 | Bentham's Calculus
Mathematics as a guide to morals

An opinion poll conducted on 3 October 1995 by CNN and the *USA Today* newspaper found that 56 per cent of Americans believed that O. J. Simpson murdered his wife Nicole and her friend Ronald Goldman. The jury, however, famously pronounced him 'not guilty'. Whether Simpson was guilty or not, it is possible that a conviction could have led to street rioting in protest. As this might have involved several deaths, Simpson's acquittal may have been for the best, assuming that he does not 're-offend'. Let's imagine a different turn of events, whereby the jury are presented with last-minute evidence that proves Simpson's guilt beyond any reasonable doubt. However, just as they are about to vote on the verdict, the jury learn that a group of armed fanatics – and this does not mean the LAPD – are poised to cause mayhem in Los Angeles should Simpson be found guilty. The members of the jury have a duty to deliver the verdict they believe to be the truth, but do they not also have a duty to prevent the deaths of innocent people should this be within their power? The answer to this moral dilemma depends upon whether the 'right' thing to do is right regardless of its consequences. To put it another way, it depends on whether morality is an end in itself or merely a means to making the world a better place. Utilitarian moralists, broadly speaking, believe the latter. For a utilitarian, the jury's dilemma is a simple one to solve. It is merely a question of doing the maths, and on this basis it is clearly better to opt for acquittal and no fatalities than to convict Simpson and face a murderous death toll.

The first utilitarian was Jeremy Bentham, who was born into a family of lawyers in London in 1748. He studied at Oxford

University before qualifying for the Bar. His father dreamed that he would become the Lord Chancellor of England, but Bentham never actually practised law, complaining that the 'Demon of Chicane' was rife in the legal system. He chose to concentrate on theory rather than practice and ultimately on the spirit of law rather than law as lawyers knew it. His approach was to delve into the moral basis of the laws that govern us. The foundation that he discovered was their utility. Bentham defined utility as 'that property in any object whereby it tends to produce pleasure, good or happiness, or to prevent the happening of mischief, pain, evil or unhappiness'. His rallying cry, which was taken up in various forms by future utilitarians, was 'the greatest happiness for the greatest number'.

By this criterion, Bentham found many institutions wanting. The established Church, abuses of the British Constitution and an inefficient penal system were all targets of his polemics. Frustration with the last of these led him to devise his famous 'Panopticon' during a stay in Russia in 1785. This was a new kind of prison, circular in shape, where the guards in the centre could keep watch on the prisoners while remaining unseen. Unfortunately Bentham failed to sell the idea to Catherine the Great, whose successors preferred to use salt mines rather than panopticons, but this did not dissuade him from spending a further twenty years and a great deal of money continuing to promote the idea, to no avail. The early nineteenth century provided a more conducive environment for Bentham and his ideas. The defeat of Napoleon in 1815 left Europe in need of a legal consultant to advise on the framing of new constitutions. Russian, German and Spanish jurists all benefited from Bentham's sage advice in this period. His wider influence on legislation, meanwhile, stretched as far as South America and the United States, where he had the ear of Presidents Adams and Madison. When he died in 1832, his remains were mummified, dressed in his clothes and, in accordance with his wishes, placed on display in a glass case in University College London. They can still be seen there today.

The utilitarian ideal captured the imagination of statesmen, but Bentham's precise method for achieving it was as eccentric as his Panopticon. Both the legislation of governments and the actions of individuals were to be subjected to the 'hedonic calculus'. The happiness or unhappiness they produced for an individual was quantified and then multiplied by the number of people who enjoyed or suffered these consequences. If the aggregate effects were good rather than bad, and a better result could not be obtained through different means, then the law or action was right and just. The hedonic calculus was a method for solving all moral dilemmas through simple addition and subtraction.

Bentham's moral system had no other god but utility. Moral rectitude was a matter of bringing about a certain state of affairs, of maximizing the prevalence of certain qualities, rather than performing duties or obeying deities. Utility itself, however, can be defined in several ways. We need to be clear about what it is before we can go out into the world and maximize it. Bentham's definition of utility was a hedonistic one: 'happiness' equals pleasure. All human beings, he thought, pursued pleasure and avoided pain wherever possible. Therefore, whatever makes most people happy, or gives them the most pleasure, is morally right. Despite this code, Bentham himself lived a simple life of hard work and moral respectability. His hedonistic desires seem to have been sated by writing for up to twelve hours a day on legal reform. This work may have sent Bentham into the throes of ecstasy, but it seems unlikely. Bentham's own lifestyle suggests that pleasure is too narrow a definition of happiness. It was left to John Stuart Mill (1806–73), the son of Bentham's pupil James Mill, to produce a more plausible definition. Mill kept the language of happiness and pleasure but made a distinction between higher and lower forms of pleasure, the former of which might include even the pursuits preferred by Bentham himself.

Whatever people seek – whatever currency is favoured for the calculus – moral action must try to make the world a better place by maximizing this currency. On the face of it, it is difficult to imagine how making the world a worse place could ever be 'doing the right thing'. Bentham's calculus is simply a mechanistic process of weighing up the good and bad consequences, and using it, he hoped, would ensure that no one was ever at a loss when confronted with a moral dilemma. True, it may be difficult to predict the effects which laws and actions will have in the future, but no one ever said that morality would be easy. When the moral project is as grand as 'maximizing the greatest good for the greatest number', the task is formidable. The distinctly non-utilitarian philosopher Immanuel Kant asserted that 'Ought implies can', which is another way of saying that there is no moral obligation to do something of which you are incapable. From a utilitarian point of view, the best state of affairs – in which every citizen is blissfully happy – may be one that puny human beings cannot achieve, but it is no less the best one for that. We may be fighting a losing battle in trying to maximize happiness, in which case, the utilitarian would say, it is simply hard luck. So long as an action produces more utility – or less pain – than anything else you could do, you are obliged to do it in order that the common good be preserved and improved.

No matter how desperate the circumstances, the utilitarian calculus will still have something to say about what you should do. Because the calculus is so versatile, one is rarely given respite from moral situations. No matter what you are doing, the likelihood is that it is morally wrong, since there will always be an orphan in the Third World to whom you could be sending food at that very moment. And if you are doing this right now, there is bound to be another starving child somewhere or other who could benefit even more from your help. Even a saint would soon suffer a moral breakdown in the face of these demands. In this case, however, the moral calculus would suggest that acting morally all the time might not be such a good idea, and the sums would be rejigged so that it is permissible sometimes to promote less than the best state of affairs. The same sleight of hand obviates the charge that we cannot expect people to be motivated by 'cold' calculations rather than 'warm' feelings. When you give your husband a birthday present, he expects that you do so because you love him. If, on the other hand, you tell him that 'giving you a present maximizes social utility', he may well ask what you have done with his *real* wife. To take another example, if a government dithers over whether or not to send aid to the victims of an earthquake, this is likely to lead to more unnecessary deaths than if relief convoys were sent right away and the questions asked afterwards. If it seems that letting warm feelings dictate one's actions sometimes leads to a better state of affairs than would cool-headed calculation, then a quick calculation would suggest that on further thought, there are occasions when the calculator should be switched off. It is in this way that utilitarianism sidesteps most of the criticisms levelled against it. Whenever its approach is deemed to be not for the best, it redefines its aims to account for this, and the problem goes away.

A deeper problem is that the sums required in the utilitarian calculus will always go awry because good and bad cannot be quantified objectively. How much suffering is a burglary worth, for example, in terms of other pains? Half the loss of a finger? A hundred insect bites? And can a death really be set against any amount of smaller pains? How can we compare one person's pleasures and pains to those of another? This leads to a further complaint: in the utilitarian calculus, nothing is sacrosanct. Utilitarianism admits no absolutes. Nothing is banned, and everything is potentially permitted according to its circumstances. In *Utilitarianism: For and Against* (1973), the English philosopher Bernard Williams (1929–) devised a thought experiment to bring out these difficulties. Imagine that you are trekking through a country that has an unenviable human rights record. You come upon a village in a jungle clearing, only to behold a firing squad taking aim at ten terrified peasants. The captain of the squad notices you appear and, concerned that a foreigner is about to witness the proceedings, hesitates to give the order to fire. You ask him what is going on. He explains that the villagers are suspected of harbouring a dissident opposition leader he has had orders to track down. So far they have refused to reveal the dissident's whereabouts, but he fancies that shooting ten of their number might change the minds of the others. He tells you that this is not an unusual occurrence but, since you are a guest in his country, he will make a special exception in this case. He will spare the lives of the ten villagers on the condition that you yourself execute a single villager. He also assures you that if you were to try any heroics, his men would shoot you immediately and they would still kill the villagers. You are caught up in the situation through no fault of your own, yet you have been asked to commit murder. This is a difficult moral dilemma, but employing a utilitarian calculus makes it 'simple' to solve. Since the death of one produces less pain than the death of ten, you are not only permitted to shoot an innocent man in this case, but are actually required to do it and will be morally reprehensible if you do not. It may not seem fair that you are asked to accept responsibility for the deaths of ten villagers when the situation was not of your own choosing, but that, as a utilitarian would say again, is tough luck.

Whether or not you would shoot in this case, the decision may become easier if the choice presented was one death against a hundred, a thousand or ten thousand innocent lives. The example forces us to admit that we are prepared to weigh one life against another. And if we do not admit this, the utilitarian can simply keep piling on the numbers until we give in and accept that the rule against taking another's life is not a moral absolute. We will also have conceded therein that the pains and pleasures of different individuals can, after all, be set against each other. However, getting rid of moral absolutes entirely is not quite so simple.

Utilitarians have an obligation not only to avoid unhappiness and harm, but also to positively promote happiness. This becomes a problem when different people define utility differently, especially when one person's pleasure consists in another's pain. Let's say that a five-hundred-strong chapter of the Ku Klux Klan are desperate to celebrate their anniversary in the traditional style. Ideally they would like to lynch someone, but they live in a state that invokes the death penalty, and they would surely receive it for such a heinous crime. Instead, they compromise on simply tarring and feathering an innocent man. The pleasure they received from this was, they tell the courtroom, indescribable. They enjoyed themselves so much that it was definitely worth the price they now have to pay. According to Bentham's hedonic calculus, they have a point. On balance, the pleasure of the five hundred perpetrators involved easily outweighs the suffering of their victim. There is no denying that the crime was good value for money in utilitarian terms, yet few would want to permit such a transaction.

It seems, then, that moral absolutes have to be built into the system at some point. When we consider the consequences of our actions, the ethical nature of the acts themselves is an integral part of the state of affairs we create. For example, lying to one's spouse to conceal adultery might keep them happy, but doing so degrades the relationship further. Using drugs to break a world record in athletics without being caught could make you world famous and, in a sense, happy, but such fame is not worth having if you can never forget that you are a cheat. Moral quantities, such as honesty or human rights, for example, must be counted along with such things as pleasure and happiness in an ethical calculus, for we cannot achieve true happiness at the cost of our moral self-respect.

17 | Hegel's Dialectic
Finding truth in conflict

As Oscar Wilde observed, the truth is rarely pure and never simple. When two opposing views clash, it is uncommon for one or the other to be found wholly right or wholly wrong. With tedious regularity, the truth of matters in dispute contains a bit of both sides. One day there will probably be an announcement on the evening news: 'Top philosophers working at Cambridge University have found . . . THE ANSWER . . . and, well, it's a bit of both.' Learning to give and take in this way may well make us better people, but it does not satisfy the absolutist in us. When we want to learn the 'truth', we do not mean to make the best of a confused job, but hope to attain the full version in all its black-and-white glory. Sometimes, before we have realized it, this is in fact what we are left with – but only ever temporarily. Two nations might squabble over a border and eventually agree to a compromise over the disputed territory. The new border is formalized in signed treaties and appears in freshly printed atlases. Only a few years then pass, however, before that border becomes the subject of a new dispute. The process begins again, and the truth that was once clear clouds over. According to the philosopher Georg Hegel, this cycle is writ large in the history of our understanding. A belief, a system, or a way of life meets its opposite and out of their struggle comes something that combines the best elements of both. Sooner or later, this synthesis too meets its opposite, and becomes another milestone in the ongoing series of culture clashes that drives human history. Hegel named this process the 'dialectic', and its goal is perfect freedom.

Hegel was born in Stuttgart in 1770, the son of a revenue officer in the civil service. He lived a relatively quiet life. The most outrageous apocryphal story associated with him is that he planted a 'liberty' tree one Sunday morning in sympathy with the French revolutionary spirit. His sedentary existence was set among great events, however, and he once avowed that if he saw any hope of success for Napoleon he would take a rifle and join him in Paris. He did not have to travel so far, though there is no record of Hegel taking up arms when Napoleon advanced into Prussia. The philosopher was even too busy working to a deadline to celebrate his hero's victory at Jena in 1806. Hegel's greatest work, *The Phenomenology of Spirit*, had garnered him a substantial cash advance that came with swingeing penalty clauses should he fail to deliver the manuscript by 13 October. The French marched into Jena to occupy the city on that very day, and Hegel was lucky that the only copy of his magnum opus arrived safely amidst the chaos. He was not so fortunate when the ensuing 'Reign of Terror' in Jena forced the closure of the university and put him out of his job as a professor. Perhaps these experiences made an impact upon his political leanings, for in his later years he became a confirmed Prussian patriot. Hegel believed that Napoleon had introduced modern, rationally conceived institutions into his backward homeland, and he later insisted that Germany had changed during his lifetime. Indeed, he claimed that his country came closer to true freedom than any other state in history. Prussia's absolutist monarchy of the time was probably as surprised by this assertion as a modern historian would be, but the ruling classes were grateful for Hegel's approval and the philosopher enjoyed the patronage of several high-ranking government officials towards the end of his life. He effectively became Prussia's state philosopher and did much to kindle German nationalism.

There are students of philosophy who approach the subject with a mission to make their preconceived ideas respectable rather than to criticize them or learn new ones. Few such students do so as successfully as Hegel. A large part of his work was concerned with formalizing the mystical intuitions of his youth. These intuitions consisted in the oneness of the universe and the belief that only the world taken in its entirety can be said to be truly real. The world's component parts exist only in relation to the whole, and it is the gradual realization of this dependence that leads us to apprehend the world as a single, perfect unity. Since we are ourselves part of the universe, the human race is the instrument by which the world becomes aware of itself. The significance of humanity had been battered by the Enlightenment, and Hegel's contemporaries seized on his ideas for their promise to restore purpose to human life. Many Enlightenment thinkers wanted reason to inform, rather than replace, religion. Hegel was among them, though he deemed religion subordinate to reason. Religion, he argued, expressed the same truths, only it did so through parable rather than directly through the intellect. As we came closer to realizing the Absolute Spirit, however, we would be able to think what previously we could merely feel and would have no further need for myths, allegories or symbolism. This would be the privilege of a civilization as attuned to philosophy as the ancient Greeks were to aesthetics. Not everyone was impressed by this vision. Hegel's great contemporary, the philosopher Arthur Schopenhauer (1788–1860), described him as a 'commonplace, inane, loathsome and ignorant charlatan' and despised the hold he exercised over young disciples. To counter Hegel's influence, Schopenhauer scheduled his lectures to clash with his rival's but was forced to terminate the course when no one turned up. Although Hegel was a poor speaker – he would cough and splutter to buy time while he leafed through copious notes to find the right turn of phrase – his lectures attracted large audiences. Schopenhauer was in the minority, and it is no exaggeration to say that Hegel took the world by storm.

As his most important ideas are not difficult to grasp, the notorious impenetrability of Hegel's writings was no bar to his influence. His method, the dialectic, is a simple one in essence and can be used to interpret an individual's experience as readily as the history of a nation. The dialectic relies on the internal contradictions, or opposites, to be found in all areas of human life. Hegel argued that all progress is achieved through the conflict of opposites, with their resolution leading humanity onwards and upwards to the realization of the Absolute Spirit, which is a perfect unity. The three stages of a dialectic are: thesis, antithesis and synthesis. The thesis might be an idea, an attitude, a civilization or a movement in history. Being incomplete in itself, each of these will sooner or later meet its antithesis. The partial truths contained in both the thesis and antithesis will then come to be embodied on a higher level in the synthesis that results from their conflict.

For a thesis, take, for example, a young recruit going off to war for the first time. He can barely control his panic at the sound of gunfire as he nears the front. At the point at which his nerves are about to break, his shame overpowers his fear and the antithesis in this case is rashness: he breaks from cover in a moment of madness and charges blindly at the enemy. If he is lucky enough to survive his wounds and reflect on his experience, he may reach the synthesis, which would be a golden mean between cowardice and rashness. In a word, bravery: an ability to meet danger with a cool head and consider calmly when to advance and when to take cover. Freedom – the currency of Hegel's dialectic – will now be better realized in his actions. He will have the ability to control himself and make a rational decision in a crisis where before he was limited by his passions. The recruit had the potential for bravery all along, but it took the conflict of his fear with his shame to bring it to expression. A modern army would prefer him to sort out this particular conflict on the training ground, and many soldiers may be able to do this. Hegel would no doubt be sceptical of these cases, however, unless, perhaps, the training ground was itself a dangerous and arduous place staffed by the very fiercest of drill instructors.

The conflicts within a dialectic need not be violent ones, even though pitched battles seem to be Hegel's favourite exemplars. In many cases of self-realization, vigorous hand-wringing will do. If we take a repressed homosexual as our thesis, the antithesis is when he or she realizes that sexual desire can be suppressed by will-power. The clash between desire and self-control leads to a synthesis, since with the power to control oneself comes also the ability to liberate oneself – to express desire deliberately rather than as a response to instinct. All being well, the result is new self-respect in which sexual preferences can be acted upon without shame. This is probably not what Hegel had in mind when he conceived of the dialectic, but his method is nothing if not flexible.

For all its personal applications, the dialectic was designed primarily for the wider canvas of history. There Hegel saw the dialectic sweeping man out of the state of nature and propelling him into the nation-state. The thesis is the unfettered behaviour of the savage, who acts as the mood takes him without thought for the consequences. In time, the savage abandons his unrestrained freedom and submits before the law and the pressures of convention. This antithesis presents him with what he perceives as tyranny. In the synthesis of these opposing conditions he becomes a citizen under the rule of law. In this new environment he is capable of much that was beyond him both as a savage and a subject. He can now understand that there is more to liberty than vulgar licence and that the law is not simply a spoilsport. Admittedly, he might have found it difficult to be so understanding in Hegel's Prussia, but the philosopher himself conceded that the course of freedom may not have reached its end. This is an important caveat, because Hegel's notion of freedom is a strange one, weighted heavily towards the state over the individual. As Bertrand Russell noted, it is not the kind that would keep you out of a concentration camp.

Hegel died in Berlin during a cholera epidemic in 1831. The future for the dialectic was far from the Absolute Knowing that he dreamed of. One of his young disciples took the method and redrew it on materialist lines. In place of the progress of the spirit, this new dialectic traced the history of man and predicted his future according to his economic conditions. The disciple was, of course, Karl Marx.

18 | Nietzsche's Hammer
Smashing our idols

At the beginning of *Twilight of the Idols*, the short volume intended as a summation of his ideas, the German philosopher Friedrich Nietzsche wrote:

This little essay is a *great declaration of war*; and regarding the sounding out of idols, this time they are not just idols of the age, but *eternal* idols, which are here touched with a hammer as with a tuning fork: there are altogether no older, no more convinced, no more puffed-up idols – and none more hollow.

Nietzsche wanted to show that the foundations on which we build our most sacred truths – our 'idols' – were a product of history. And the particular history in question, he believed, was a sorry tale of self-deception. He proposed that we should not use reason to comprehend life and nature, but the power of decision. This is not because we thereby gain a clearer picture of the world – though in fact we do – but because to act in this way is to be true to our nature and to our 'Will to Power'. Nietzsche describes the Will to Power as 'an insatiable desire to manifest power; or as the employment and exercise of power, as a creative drive'. This, he held, was a faculty stunted in modern man. Moreover, he believed its state of degeneracy to be so advanced that nothing short of the total destruction of our value system was required before we could reawaken our Will to Power in its former glory. Only then would the world be inhabitable for the *Übermensch* – the superman.

Friedrich Nietzsche was born in 1844 into a devout Protestant family in the German town of Röcken bei Lützen, near Leipzig.

His father was a Lutheran minister, as were his grandfathers, but the family profession was to come to an abrupt end with Nietzsche. Nietzsche's father died when he was four years old, his younger brother six months later. His family moved to Naumburg, where Nietzsche lived as the only male in a household of five women. When he was fourteen, he won a scholarship to Schulpforta, Germany's most prominent Protestant boarding school, where he excelled in the classics. He entered the University of Bonn in 1864 as a theology and philology student, though he concentrated exclusively on the latter. Falling into disputes with two of his professors, he transferred to the University of Leipzig a year later to study under the classical scholar Friedrich Wilhelm Ritschl. In Leipzig he met the composer Richard Wagner and carved his own reputation so successfully that he was offered a professorship at the University of Basel in Switzerland. He was only twenty-four and had yet to complete his doctorate. This rise was interrupted by military service, for which he was posted to the cavalry company of a Prussian artillery regiment. While attempting to leap into the saddle of his horse one day, he fell to the ground and suffered a severe chest injury. This was not the end of Nietzsche's troubles with the army. When he volunteered as a medical orderly during the Franco-Prussian War in 1870, he contracted dysentery and diphtheria within weeks, from which he never properly recovered. He was forced to resign his professorship through ill health in 1879 and thereafter lived in virtual solitude, wandering between Italy, the Swiss Alps and the French Riviera.

For the rest of his working life, Nietzsche was tormented by powerful headaches and deteriorating vision. The first decade of his isolation, however, was also his most fertile period, producing *Thus Spake Zarathustra* (1883–5) and *The Antichrist* (withheld from publication until 1895), as well as *Twilight of the Idols* (1889). Though he lamented that few contemporaries would understand his greatness, he was not shy of advertising it. Three chapters of *Ecce Homo*, completed in 1888, were entitled 'Why I am so Clever', 'Why I am so Wise' and 'Why I write such Good Books'. In Turin on 3 January 1889, Nietzsche saw a horse being whipped by a coachman and threw his arms around its neck to protect the animal. He collapsed weeping, and this conspicuously un-Nietzschean expression of pity marked the beginning of eleven years of insanity which ended with his death in 1900. It is tempting to attribute his breakdown to the force of his ideas and two rejections in love. But we should also consider the tertiary symptoms of syphilis and Nietzsche's use of chloral hydrate as a sedative. In any case, he was to suffer further indignity after his death through the actions of his sister and nurse, Elizabeth. She had earlier worked with her anti-Semitic husband, Bernard Forster, to establish an Aryan colony in Paraguay. As her brother's literary executor, she re-edited Nietzsche's notes and forged others to reflect her own views while refusing public access to the archive. When Adolf Hitler came to power she gave the Nazi regime Nietzsche's posthumous blessing. The *Übermensch*, however, was a human type, not a racial type. Nietzsche was not anti-Semitic – indeed, Wagner's anti-Semitism eventually helped to wear out Nietzsche's patience with the composer. He also admired the Arabs and Japanese for their noble spirit, while holding the Germans in contempt. He deemed his own people second only to the 'idiotic' English in degeneracy. Patriotic, nationalistic and racist, the Nazis would certainly have been despised by Nietzsche. Nietzsche is today widely acknowledged to be the finest ever writer of German prose. That said, to read any of his major works is to be exposed to insights of genius and the rantings of a maniac in equal measure.

Nietzsche believed that truth was never something we *discover* about the world – which is inherently chaotic in any case – but something imposed upon it by an individual's 'will to truth'. This is the ego's striving for permanence at the moment it imposes order on chaos. Our systems of understanding the world are nothing more than memorials to the will of philosophers. They were not constructed according to logic, but rather by a process akin to artistic creation. The superman is able to face the chaos around him and still impose order upon it through the force of his Will to Power. If this seems a capricious outlook, the notion of 'objective' truth is no better, Nietzsche argues. Since such false ideas as God's love for his creations give us comfort whereas the facts are often painful, the unconditional preference of scientists for 'truth' over 'untruth' is no more than a moral prejudice. It is even a self-defeating one, for in the course of the history that Nietzsche recounts, our belief in a 'real' world independent of our perceptions has turned inwards and negated its own foundation. The story begins with Plato, who originally conceived of a 'true' world that was within the grasp of the wise and virtuous. This was then incorporated into Christianity and held out as a promise to the rest of us in the form of heaven. With the philosophy of Immanuel Kant, the character of the ideal world became unknowable to human powers of apprehension, but at least it still existed. Later still, philosophers asked how human beings could possibly be expected to derive guidance from something that was unknowable, and so the 'true' world became, as Nietzsche put it, 'useless and superfluous'. With the world of 'truth' went also that of appearances, for neither is the way things appear a truth 'in-itself' – even the most uncontroversial 'facts' are subject to interpretation. Furthermore, Nietzsche accepted that this idea too – his own – was itself only an interpretation.

Nietzsche did not think that one interpretation was as good as any other, however, for he held truth to be a moral quantity. The truths and interpretations of happy, healthy, strong individuals were preferable to those of the weak and abject. To his disgust, he found that the dominant values of the Western world seemed to have derived from the latter. How did the weak achieve this, for they are surely no match for the lion among men with his indomitable Will to Power? Nietzsche's answer is that mediocrity prevailed through force of numbers. By banding together under the Jewish faith, the 'slaves' who followed Jesus Christ overthrew the morality of their 'masters' and replaced aristocratic virtues with the language of resentment. Christianity damned the noble, beautiful and powerful to the fires of a fictional hell while the earth was bequeathed to the meek and the lame. This creative act of the slaves was not a celebration of their new-found freedom, but merely a reaction against the values of their former masters. These values were corrupted and inverted: self-confidence, for example, became 'arrogance', and the inability to exact revenge on one's enemies became the virtue of 'forgiveness'. Healthy pride was replaced by humility, and fruitful competition gave way to charity.

Thus the moral age began, for the aristocrats had had no need of rules to constrain them or punishments to coerce them. Morality is the province not of the individual, but of the 'herd', which foists its notions of 'good' and 'evil' on us without allowing us to create our own. The individualism that survives is tarred with discontentment. Defiance of the herd prompts pangs of guilt and conscience that suppress the free play of our instincts. The prevalence of guilt destroys our self-respect and makes us no better than a 'camel', a status we have accepted for want of an easy life. What we achieve is an illusion of ease, however, for 'Under conditions of peace, the warlike man attacks himself'. With the denial of 'natural' virtues came the denial of the world of the senses through the degenerate philosophy of Greek Platonism. The latter account applied even to the self, separating a person from his or her actions and making 'good' or 'evil' intentions possible where before there was only the immediate venting of the will. Nietzsche exhorts us to take nihilism to the enemy by destroying his values and creating new ones that are faithful to our Will to Power. This requires a creative will and not a logical mind.

Nietzsche was not unduly worried that the means he used to attack other philosophers could also be applied to his own ideas. He was not interested in engaging other thinkers in a battle of logical wits. Truth, as we normally understand the term, was not strictly the subject matter of his philosophy – since he thought that the ability to create and destroy truth preceded the mythical ability to discern it. His ideas thereby undercut those of his opponents rather than engaging with them. He philosophizes with a 'hammer' used to 'sound out' idols, 'which are touched with a hammer as with a tuning fork' until the reverberations reduce them to dust. An idea becomes an idol when an expression of our will to truth masquerades as an objective truth about the world. To take things this far is not only to deceive oneself, but also to insult the creative drive by which we fashion truths. In doing so we elevate our ideas only by debasing ourselves. A 'healthy' philosopher, by contrast, is happy to carve his truths out of appearances and leave them at that – at the level of instinct – because self-doubt does not compel him to seek a status for his truths higher than his own affirmation of them.

'All creators are hard,' Nietzsche wrote, 'and it must seem bliss to you to impress your hand on millennia as on wax, bliss to write on the will of millennia as on bronze – harder than bronze, nobler than bronze. Only the noblest is altogether hard.' The Will to Power seems to be something so hard that there is nothing harder with which to fashion it. If only there were such a substance. Because force of will patently cannot conquer all, Nietzsche's exhortations represent an attitude to the human condition rather than any real plan for changing it. He famously declared that 'Whatever does not kill me, makes me stronger.' But even if we accept that suffering is sometimes good for us, it remains rather irrational to desire it for its own sake on the grounds that it cannot be avoided. Nietzsche avows to transform every 'It was' into an 'I willed it thus!' He asks us to become 'yea-sayers, saying yes to all that has happened and will happen'. What is the difference, however, between this response to the world and that of the slave who rejoices when his master beats him, claiming that that was exactly what he desired all along? A sense of humour is a fine stick with which to attack our adversaries, but joining them – as Nietzsche effectively proposes – is quite different to beating them.

'I do not point to the evil and pain of existence with the finger of reproach,' Nietzsche professed, 'but rather entertain the hope that life may one day become more evil and more full of suffering than it has ever been.' This makes for a very strange form of life affirmation. Nietzsche teaches us not to yield in the face of adversity; the celebration of suffering he advocates is more akin to cooperating with our adversaries than opposing and defeating them. Far better to *retreat* to the high moral ground than to claim, like Nietzsche, that one has found it in the depths. If a crisis were not itself an evil, we could not talk of 'overcoming' it. Even if calamities are sent to 'test' us, as it were, one would think we should rejoice only when the problem is solved. When reading Nietzsche, we have to ask ourselves the honest question: do we or do we not enjoy pain? Stoicism or 'yea-saying' may make one noble, but there is no reason why an angry rebellion against one's lot cannot achieve the same end. That is not to say it is noble to whinge and whine in the face of suffering – nor that we should exercise the denial of which Nietzsche accuses humanity – but that, though we must accept what comes to us and make the best of it, we do not also have to like it. If you lose both your legs in a road accident, learning to cope with your disability is an admirable thing, but it is *your* admirable thing. It is certainly no thanks to the drunk driver who ran over you. Though you may greet every day with a smile and never allow your predicament to conquer you, this does not annul your grounds for reasonable complaint, let alone legal proceedings. It is one thing to say that how we react to experiences is wholly within our own power, but the nature of our experiences once they have occurred is clearly often beyond it. Like other forms of madness, Nietzschean megalomania is of little help to the human condition.

In telling us of the potential for all adversity to be turned to one's advantage, Nietzsche was himself party to a myth, one created by the strong rather than the herd. He was right that life's losers often deny personal responsibility for events and overestimate the role of bad luck in their downfall. But what he did not acknowledge was that those who are successful in life are themselves only too ready to accept the credit 'due' to them and naturally downplay the role of luck in their achievements. Protesting that the rest of humanity could have done better with their opportunities is the means by which the strong and healthy assuage their guilt at their own good fortune. This does not by any means apply to everyone with a high salary, a large house and a sports car. But rather than feeling genuine sympathy for, say, poorly paid workers in the Third World, it is so much easier on one's ego to think that they can improve their lot through their own efforts, or that such benefits will accrue to their children and grandchildren. Such individuals in fact moved among the herd all along – they were the ones telling us that our sufferings would be seen aright in heaven. If Christianity is moral slavery, then it was a bondage indoctrinated into the slaves by the *Übermensch* rather than one they constructed themselves. Now that God is 'dead', as Nietzsche says, and we no longer believe unquestioningly in heaven, things have not changed very much. Far from demolishing this 'idol', Nietzsche himself helped to maintain the status quo by telling us that our tragedies do not matter greatly because we can always overcome them. Just when our greatest source of self-oppression was crumbling, Nietzsche arrived to erect a new one. In place of surrender to evil and adversity, he gave us collaboration with it.

19 | The Young Wittgenstein's Mirror
What can be shown, but not said

The finest novelists show us what the worst ones can only tell us. Emotions best display their power when they are exhibited – in fiction as in life – for their value is apt to be lost in the telling. As a young man, the philosopher Ludwig Wittgenstein argued that this held for all the truths, both intellectual and moral, that thinkers sought to uncover. Philosophy was a mirror that could reflect the world, but not one that could articulate it. The essence of the world, and the essence of our thoughts, he believed, cannot be talked about but only shown. The early twentieth century was a time when philosophers rewrote the problems of philosophy as problems of language. Over a hundred years earlier, Immanuel Kant had realized that before we can understand the world, we must understand the faculties of perception and processes of thought through which it is mediated. Wittgenstein took a step further back and argued that, since all understanding takes place through language, studying the latter will yield the most accurate picture of the world. Philosophical questions have to be framed in words, so if you find the limits of language you thereby find the limits of what can be asked and answered in philosophy.

The youngest of eight children, Wittgenstein was born in Vienna in 1889. His family was one of the richest in Europe. His father Karl was an iron and steel magnate and one of the Austro-Hungarian Empire's foremost captains of industry. Until he was fourteen, Wittgenstein received his education at the family home – a centre of music and culture that numbered the composer Johannes Brahms among its frequent visitors. All Wittgenstein's siblings were talented individuals, but instability was as evident in the family as genius, and three of his four brothers committed suicide. In 1908, Wittgenstein went to Manchester University in England to study aeronautics, a pursuit that led him to mathematics and thence to philosophy. He left Manchester and engineering and sought out Bertrand Russell in Cambridge, where he became the philosopher's protégé. Within two years, Russell realized that his pupil would one day surpass him. Wittgenstein claimed that Russell's assurance of his talents saved him from the thoughts of worthlessness that might have led him to suicide. It could not have been quite enough, however, for on the outbreak of the First World War Wittgenstein enlisted in the Austro-Hungarian army. Through the intensity of the experience, he believed, he would 'turn into a different person'. The army placed him in administrative jobs, but he applied again and again to be sent to the front, where he was eventually decorated several times for bravery. He continued his study of philosophy in the trenches, writing the notes that would become the only book to be published in his lifetime, the *Tractatus Logico-Philosophicus*.

Wittgenstein had the kind of disregard for material comfort that only an aristocrat could possess. On inheriting a fortune, he gave most of it away to his sisters on the grounds that, as they were already rich, it would damage them the least. He encouraged his working-class students to give up philosophy and return to the life of labour, and once even went as far as applying for Soviet citizenship so that he could live as a peasant. The Russian authorities informed him that they had quite enough peasants already, but that they would be pleased for him to take up a teaching post at one of their universities. He declined the offer, and lived frugally for the rest of his life. In 1920 – two years before the *Tractatus* was finally published – Wittgenstein retired to the Alps to become an elementary school teacher. He was only thirty-one, but he believed that he had already solved the problems of philosophy in the seventy-five pages of his first book. Nine years later he returned to Cambridge to solve them all over again.

While serving on the Eastern Front, Wittgenstein heard about a court case in which a model street was presented to explain the events that had led to a car accident. This gave him the idea that our words functioned like the toy cars and dolls in the model – organized to build up a picture of reality. All representational systems, he argued consequently, must work by way of such analogies. Though our words do not resemble the objects to which they refer – they are merely arbitrary symbols that we have agreed to use to denote certain objects – resemblance does arise when we look at the relationships between words in a sentence and objects in a state of affairs. The relation of a statement to a state of affairs is like that of a scale map to the terrain it represents. Though the map is, of course, much smaller than the terrain, this does not matter since the distances between locations drawn on it are analogous to those between their counterparts in the real world.

For language to be possible, Wittgenstein reasoned, the form or structure of sentences must be the same as that exhibited by states of affairs in the world. Structures in the world must be mirrored in the structures of the language we use to talk about them. Just as a complicated state of affairs can be broken down into its parts, language can be analysed into simpler components. Nouns represent simple objects in the world, and the way they are conjoined in a sentence represents how the corresponding objects referred to stand in relation to one another. Where objects stand in spatial relations, words stand in logical ones. This shared structure is what we recognize when we understand that the statement, 'The cat is on the mat', refers to *that* cat which is on *that* mat. It is as if we line up a statement against the world like a ruler or a transparent grid to see if the two match. When they do match, we have said something that is true.

The relationships between objects in the world are not themselves additional objects. When the cat sits on the mat, there is a cat, a mat and the relation between them – there is no third object, which is the cat's-being-on-the-mat. Likewise, the logical relations between words in a statement are not extra words, but are shown in the structure of the things we say. This is important because it means that the relationship between our language and the world it pictures cannot itself be stated in language. There is one thing in the world that a picture cannot depict – and that is itself. It cannot depict what it is about itself that makes it a picture. If we were to take a painting of a pipe and write on it, 'This is a picture of a pipe', we would be going outside the pictorial form. If, on the other hand, we were to regard the writing as just another part of the painting, it would stand in need of interpretation just as the rest of the picture does. We would need to inscribe a further statement on the painting to say what the writing was doing – and then we would be back to the same problem again. This is because truth is not intrinsic to pictures; rather, it is something a picture gains by virtue of its relation to something else – something *outside* itself – namely, the state of affairs that it represents. Whatever goes on within the picture is just more picture – which we can then hold up against the world to see if it is accurate or not. The addendum 'This is a picture of a pipe' would have to be similarly held up. Needless to say, we cannot hold a picture up against itself, for this would be no different to simply looking at the picture.

Since language is a form of depiction, the same limitations apply to words, which may represent anything in reality, but cannot represent what they have in common with reality in order to be able to represent it. If we tried to do this with words, we would only produce more language, just as we only produce more picture by writing directly on to the painting. The question of meaningfully assessing words – as philosophers are supposed to do all the time – therefore cannot arise.

Yet if language is the means through which we understand the world, it seems reasonable to imagine that there could be a better one. Wittgenstein's theory applies, however, not just to English or French, but to all possible tongues. The rules he codified applied to any language that relies on representation for its intelligibility. So if we wanted to see how well our words map on to the world, or how well our philosophical concepts describe reality, we would be unable to – since we would need to do it from a position outside of our system of representation. We would need to be able to look at that system on the one hand, and the world on the other, but no such standpoint is available to us when we are using language itself.

Just as we cannot talk of an area that cannot be mapped, so we cannot talk of states of affairs that cannot be represented in language. Conversely, just as a map of nowhere does not represent anything, utterances that do not refer to anything in the world are nonsensical. As Wittgenstein's contemporary, Frank Ramsey, remarked in his review of the *Tractatus*, 'What can't be said can't be said, and it can't be whistled either.' The final sentence of the *Tractatus* reads, 'Whereof one cannot speak, thereof one must be silent.' As a work of philosophy that describes the essence of language, however, the *Tractatus* itself is clearly far from silent on these very things. Ordinary language exhibits its structure, and that of the world, by showing it to us. The *Tractatus*, on the other hand, has attempted to state explicitly what that structure is and, in so doing, has rendered itself meaningless on its own terms. Wittgenstein explains his position thus:

My propositions serve as elucidations in the following way: anyone who understands me eventually recognises them as nonsensical, when he has used them – as steps – to climb up beyond them. (He must, so to speak, throw away the ladder after he has climbed up it.)

He must transcend these propositions, and then he will see the world aright.

Wittgenstein admits that he has failed to say anything meaningful – he has *told* us nothing – but in doing so he has demonstrated, or *shown* us, something very important:

When the answer cannot be put into words, neither can the question be put into words.

The *riddle* does not exist.

If a question can be framed at all, it is also possible to answer it.

Since the *Tractatus* shows that the answers to the problems of philosophy cannot be put into words, it demonstrates that the questions were misguided all along. Wittgenstein continues,

The solution of the problem of life is seen in the vanishing of the problem.

(Is not this the reason why those who have found after a long period of doubt that the sense of life became clear to them have been unable to say what constituted that sense?)

Apropos the picture theory, the meaning of something always lies outside that thing, in the way that a picture obviously must be located outside that which it depicts (were it internal to its subject, then it would be that very thing and not a picture of it at all). If we are to treat our existence as a sign that has a meaning, then the meaning of life will lie outside life. To attempt to speak of the problem of life – or of ethical or aesthetic values – is to run up against the walls of language. But in charting the interior of the cage, Wittgenstein hinted, the outside makes itself manifest. In a letter to the writer Ludwig von Ficker, he professed:

I wanted to write that my work consisted of two parts: of the one which is here, and of everything which I have *not* written. And precisely this second part is the important one. For the Ethical is delimited from within, as it were, by my book; and I'm convinced that *strictly* speaking, it can ONLY be delimited in this way. In brief, I think: All of that which many are babbling about today, I have delved in my book by remaining silent about it.

The limitations of explicit assertion are evident in everyday life. For example, if I promise to be home early from work, I cannot convince someone that I really mean it simply by reiterating the fact – as if sincerity is another statement to be tagged on to the first. Moreover, I have not kept my promise by announcing 'Here I am!' when I get home. By arriving on time I *show* my partner that what I *said* was true. Neither is my sincerity an intention, like a mental note that I make to myself – for this will count for little if I dawdle on my way to the station. Where talk is cheap, thoughts are worthless. When Wittgenstein applies this analysis to philosophy – where thoughts are worth a great deal – he reveals the similar limitations of any statement that purports to express 'great' truths such as the nature of God or the value of human life. Whenever there is representation, the most important truths will be ones that can only be shown and not stated. However, there is more to language than representation, as Wittgenstein himself discovered in the second phase of his intellectual career.

20 | The Older Wittgenstein's Games
Escaping from the fly-bottle

When he was older, Ludwig Wittgenstein gave up propounding philosophical theories. Indeed, his entire later thought consists of a compendium of tools and methods for getting rid of them. He no longer believed that philosophy was a search for truth (not even a futile one), but held that it should concentrate on clearing up the confusions it created. Thinking philosophically will either lead us from nonsense back into sense, or will show us that we are at a dead end and should cease to pursue a particular line of questioning. Philosophy is a search for clarity rather than an attempt to uncover new truths about life and the world. Its purpose, in Wittgenstein's words, is to 'show the fly the way out of the fly-bottle'. Like doctors researching vaccines, philosophers should seek to abolish themselves. When done properly, philosophy 'leaves everything as it is', for neither theorizing nor discovering new facts are its business, he believed. Wittgenstein's approach is not to propose theories, but instead to analyse and describe in detail what is going on when we use language. His advice is: 'Don't think, look!'

Wittgenstein was disappointed with his experiences as an elementary school teacher in Austria in the 1920s. He urged his pupils to better themselves, but was constantly frustrated by the low expectations of their parents. He did not help his case by enforcing draconian discipline in class, regularly 'boxing the ears' of children (girls and boys alike) who failed to meet his exacting standards in mathematics. Fortunately, the idea of a new philosophy had been gestating in him during this time. In 1929, at the age of thirty-nine, he returned to Cambridge to teach at Trinity College, whereupon his admirer the great economist John Maynard Keynes wrote to his wife, 'Well, God has arrived. I met him on the 5.15 train.' The room in which Wittgenstein lived and taught was furnished with a bed, a sink and a deck-chair, and students had to bring in more deck-chairs if they wanted a seat during his lectures. He gave up his professorship in 1947 so that he could concentrate on writing, much of which he completed in retreat in rural Ireland. There he was regarded as a local eccentric. While one farmer banned him from his land because he 'frightened the cows', he seems to have learned during this time how to literally charm birds from the trees. Two days after his sixtieth birthday in 1951, Wittgenstein died from prostate cancer in Cambridge. His last words were, reportedly: 'Tell them I've had a wonderful life.'

As in his youth, Wittgenstein continued in later life to argue that philosophical problems were to be tackled through a study of language. But the task now was not to show how our language mirrors the world and delivers truth. Truth, instead of a quality that is present or absent from our beliefs, is rather an activity which is simply performed or not performed. An action, unlike a statement, cannot be true or false, but it can be appropriate or inappropriate according to the context in which it is executed. Even statements, however, are to be regarded as actions in Wittgenstein's later philosophy. Statements are correct not when they correspond with the reality they are attempting to mirror, but when we are using language correctly – that is, when the words in the statement are consistent with the rules and conventions of the system, the 'language game', of which they are a part. To understand a word or concept is to be able to use it according to the appropriate rules. If you break these rules, you are not 'wrong' as such, but are not playing that particular game. It is a rule of the ethics language game, for example, that if you believe that something is right, you will feel moved to act upon it (or at least think that you should). If you were playing tennis and someone pointed out to you that you were playing rather badly, you could answer that you did not mind and that you were not really interested in playing any better. But if someone told you that you were *acting* badly, you could not agree with them and then say that you were not interested in improving your behaviour. If you answered in this way, then it would show that you did not really understand what the words 'right' and 'wrong' meant. You would be ignorant not of ethical truths, but of the rules according to which ethical statements must be made in order to qualify as ethical. According to Wittgenstein, to know something is to know *how* to do something rather than to know *that* something is the case.

However, before a language game can be played it has to be viable. All viable language games – that is to say, those that can be played at all – must meet certain conditions. For one, they have to be shared activities. The rules must be publicly available, or we would never be able to learn them. This goes even for the language of things we normally think of as irreducibly private, since a child can learn only from the language and behaviour that he or she observes. We might think that whether or not one is in pain, for example, is a matter for the individual to settle. Yet children learn the word 'pain' from hearing others speak of it when they burn their fingers or stub their toes, and seeing how people react when they use the term. If 'pain' referred purely to a sensation, on the other hand, and had no necessary connection with writhing, yelping and swearing, then an adult English speaker – let's call her 'Martha' – who used the word in the normal way might have been misusing it all her life without knowing it. Perhaps every single time that she has seen someone jumping up and down, claiming to be feeling 'pain', they have in fact been faking it to gain sympathy. Martha has still learned how to use the word 'pain' – even if she is not always quite canny enough to know when others are using it disingenuously. Assuming that her tormentors have had their fun and now want to put her out of (or maybe into) her misery, how can they go about this? They cannot show Martha their sensations of pain, as these are supposed to be essentially private (this is supposedly how the fakers were able to fool her). Neither would it work if they jabbed her with a sharp stick and said, 'That's pain' – since they would have no way of knowing, save for her outward behaviour, whether she feels the same sensation as they do when jabbed.

Since outward behaviour – our reactions and speech – is the only thing we have to go on, it must be all we need in order to teach someone how to use a term. Even if telepathy exists, many will testify that that was not how they learned their vocabularies. Neither do we know our words innately, as there are thousands of different languages in the world – all of which have to be learned through a long process of observation. Not only must the rules of a language game be shared by a community of users, but they cannot be the province only of a select group of individuals known as philosophers. For Wittgenstein, the 'public' means the general public. It is ordinary language users who already have the answers, for they are able to employ terms in language games without difficulty. Only when they misuse their language do they become philosophers and stand in need of Wittgensteinian therapy to lead them out of the fly-bottle.

All games have rules that can be followed or broken, and it must be possible for us to know when we are breaking them, for otherwise there would be no discernible difference between playing the game and not playing it. According to Wittgenstein's 'private language argument', the thing that determines whether or not one is playing by the rules must lie outside oneself, for otherwise it would be too easy to break the rules unwittingly. If following a rule correctly consisted merely in *feeling* that you were doing so, you could have the feeling even though you were in fact breaking the rule. In effect, there would be no difference between following a rule and merely *thinking* that you were following it. In the real world, of course, you would soon be reminded of the rules if you picked up the ball and ran with it during a game of soccer.

Protesting that you thought you were doing the right thing would not get you very far with the referee. You may have been confused and thought you were playing a game of rugby or American football, but even in this case you were abiding by certain rules, albeit not those of your team-mates on the playing field. The meaningfulness of our words and actions, the fact that they follow rules, presumes that a world exists outside one's own mind. Rules, it seems, cannot be given to oneself but must be imposed from without. Though the truth may be a matter of convention, it cannot be a convention of one.

Though the rules of every language game lie in the public sphere, this does not necessarily make learning them an easy task. Every rule is subject to interpretation and, no matter how good the teaching, misunderstandings remain possible. Rules may be learned through observation, but it is not possible to observe every application of a given rule, such as every single move the king might make in a game of chess. We show a beginner how the piece moves by shifting one space here and one space there, but he might not realize that it cannot be moved off the board, for example. Our explanation cannot hope to cover every mistake he might make, yet most of us have little difficulty in learning the rules of chess or any other game. This is partly because the rules are public, and so others can tell when we are making a mistake and correct our errors. But it is also because certain errors are more common than others. Some, such as eating the pieces one captures, are so rare that we usually do not need to point them out to beginners in advance. This is because of experiences we share as humans before the language game begins. We are able to communicate with one another easily because we share a 'form of life'. This form of life is one that might not be familiar to other creatures, such as cats – with whom communication is difficult if not impossible. As Wittgenstein puts it in

Philosophical Investigations, 'If a lion could speak, we would not be able to understand him.'

This is not to say that the same rules cannot lead to different conclusions. If someone believes he has been abducted by aliens, when we know very well that he merely received a knock on the head and spent a week unconscious in hospital, he could have reached his conclusion by using the same criteria as us: for example, the strange scars on his head and the memory loss. If we tell him that the operation to repair the wounds caused the scarring while amnesia is a normal reaction to sedative drugs, he might come round to our point of view. If he does not, then he is no longer playing the evidence game. In this case, we cannot say that his belief is wrong, as it is not the kind that can be right or wrong. The 'abductee' may, of course, *think* he is right and complain that he has overwhelming 'evidence' for his case, but it is not for him to decide. This does not mean that the majority opinion is always the correct one – language games are not a theatre of political power – for we could imagine our abductee convincing a lot of Americans that alien abductions do indeed take place. (Indeed, on current statistics, this seems to be exactly what can and does happen.)

Philosophical problems arise when 'language goes on holiday', as Wittgenstein put it. We can be 'bewitched' by our way of talking so that when I say that I have a plan 'in mind', I begin to think of the mind as a box with contents. I am then tempted to ask 'meaningless' or 'confused' questions such as 'Where are these contents held?' and 'Where is my mind located?' One of the oldest philosophical confusions Wittgenstein identified comes from the assumption that the meaning of a word is the object to which it refers. As this was the basis of the *Tractatus*, it was Wittgenstein's own oldest confusion too. 'Bucephalus' seems to refer to the steed of Alexander the Great, and 'Black Bess' to the horse ridden by Dick Turpin. So what creature does the word 'horse' refer to? Plato's answer was that it named a perfect horse that galloped through the perfect fields of a higher world. Other thinkers more soberly suggested that it referred to an object in the mind rather than in the world – to the *idea* of a horse. But if meaning is a question of use rather than of reference, there is no need for the word 'horse' to name anything at all, so long as that does not stop us from using the term in an everyday way. To employ a Wittgensteinian metaphor, when an architect sinks piles into the ground to lay the foundations for his house, they do not need to reach solid rock, but merely to provide a base firm enough to support the building. If the building stands, then the foundations are good enough. They may even be allowed to shift a little if this does not compromise the integrity of the structure. In fact, our language shifts a great deal over time. New types of language games come into existence while others become obsolete or are forgotten. As Wittgenstein says, 'Our language can be seen as an ancient city: a maze of little streets and squares, and of houses with additions from various periods; and this surrounded by a multitude of new boroughs with straight regular streets and uniform houses . . . And to imagine a language means to imagine a form of life.'

Just as meaning is not fixed, neither is it singular. We are able to group a plethora of different things together under the name 'horse' even when there is no one quality which they all share. Bucephalus, Black Bess, the Trojan Horse, and the pommel horse used by gymnasts are not linked by one immutable essence, but by certain 'family resemblances'. Such groupings are not correct or incorrect: we can only say that they are used or not used by speakers at large. Someone compiling a dictionary needs to take a broad view of the different kinds of horses, but this does not stop a community of race-horse breeders from limiting their definition to the flesh-and-blood variety for their own purposes. Notions of truth and falsehood may then be established within the confines of the equine language game, but the game itself cannot be true or false: it is merely played or not played. This is similar to the way in which there are no good or bad fiction genres, but only good or bad works within a genre. It makes no sense to say that science fiction is better than murder mystery, only that a book may be good or bad science fiction or good or bad murder mystery. We can make the latter judgement because there are rules internal to each genre by which we discern value. Where there are no rules – as in the visual arts today – there can be no ascribing of good or bad. It is not that such practices as contemporary art are valueless, merely that value (or a lack of it) is not the sort of quality that can be ascribed to its products.

Wittgenstein realized that reason terminates in action, and that explanation must end in description or else it will never end at all. When we make decisions, for example, we choose on the basis of factors that we did not choose. And when we offer reasons for our actions, we cannot explain one reason by reference to another and then another, and another ad infinitum. Sooner or later we will alight on something that just 'is the case' or represents 'the way we are'. But the fact that our language games are as they are is not quite as arbitrary as Wittgenstein suggests. Our linguistic practices – just like our other practices – are there to help us survive in our environment, to help us act successfully or to further our interests. They have evolved and adapted to fit our needs, and it makes sense to ask whether another game could meet those needs more efficiently. The question is whether or not these needs are our concern, as they lie outside the language in which Wittgenstein believed we were trapped. Since we do seem to care about them – as is shown by there being a history of philosophical thought – there are grounds to suspect that a very real part of ourselves precedes language. This is an empirical matter, however, and not one that Wittgenstein would judge the province of philosophers. Nevertheless, in so far as philosophers have continued to make progress since Wittgenstein's death in 1951, it is largely because they have not taken this prohibition too seriously.

21 | Popper's Dolls
How to be one's own best enemy

One day a child asks his mother if his toys come to life when the household is asleep. Although she tells him that this is unlikely, he is unconvinced and hatches a plan to catch the toys at play. At first he lies in bed with his eyes tightly shut, listening carefully for telltale sounds. He holds his breath but fails to hear the patter of tiny plastic feet, let alone the xylophones of the Nutcracker Suite. Pretending to have fallen asleep, he leaps out of bed and switches the light on. 'Gotcha!' he shouts, but the rag dolls and tin soldiers have not moved. Hmm, he thinks, these toys are too quick for me. The boy instructs his dog to stand guard all night and to bark should any of the toys so much as twitch. Rover obediently sits up until morning, but his master enjoys a full night of unbroken sleep. The boy now puts his faith in modern technology and the following night sets up the family's brand-new camcorder in front of the toybox. The next morning he is again disappointed as the playback reveals only the motionless poses of the soldiers and the fixed expressions of the dolls. He asks his mother for further advice over breakfast, but she tells him that trip-wires are not allowed in her house and that he will have to wait for Christmas if he wants to have infrared sensors installed. In that case, he says, he will be locking his toybox from now on.

The philosopher Sir Karl Popper would not have been short of advice for the boy, though he was apt to show little patience with the child's counterparts in the adult world. Popper was born in 1902 in Vienna. As a student he was enthusiastic about the *de rigueur* ideas of Marx and the psychoanalytic theories of Freud and Adler. His intellectual tastes were transformed in

1919, however, when he attended a lecture on relativity delivered by Einstein. Popper realized that Einstein possessed a critical spirit entirely lacking in the thought of Marx and Freud. Whereas the latter duo were, thought Popper, greedy for confirmation of their theories, Einstein was brave enough to construct a hypothesis that risked falsification. Unaccompanied by the usual voluminous literature of corroborating instances, the theory of relativity instead made clear predictions that could be put to the test and, if found to be incorrect, falsify it. This critical spirit infused Popper's adventures in fields as diverse as quantum mechanics and evolutionary theory, and informed his great refutation of Marxism, *The Open Society*, published in 1945. As is often the case, Popper's political views sat somewhat oddly with his everyday methods of dealing with people: he tolerated no evasion in discussions. An American visitor who attended one of the philosopher's seminars compared the experience to appearing before the House Un-American Activities Committee. The philosopher Bryan Magee (1930–) said that his chief first impression of Popper was of an intellectual aggressiveness such as he had never encountered before. Magee added that the great man put him in mind of a 'blowtorch', at least until he had mellowed with age. Even Popper's closest friends acknowledged that, despite his liberal political views, he seemed unable to accept differences of opinion. As Professor of Logic and Scientific Method at the London School of Economics, meanwhile, Popper earned among students and colleagues the nickname 'the totalitarian liberal'. It might be offered in his defence that if Popper did not practise the pluralism and tolerance he preached, this was because he was acting in accordance with his wider philosophical views. Popper came to teach that we should worry less whether our views can be proved correct than that they can be proved incorrect. He was consistent in that he directed his ferocity towards undermining the views of dissenters rather than dogmatically bolstering his own opinions.

Popper saw that those who seek proof for their theories seem destined never to be satisfied. According to the traditional view, however, this is how science operates – by the method of induction. The scientist observes the world around him and notes patterns and regularities. He then works towards a theory that explains these phenomena and predicts others like them. On a visit to a lake, a zoologist might notice that every swan he sees happens to be white. He then forms the hypothesis that all swans are snowy white, and his theory gains greater credence each time he observes another white swan. Unfortunately, he would need to observe every living swan in order to confirm his theory. According to Popper's argument, the zoologist's time would be better spent searching for a black swan – for if such a bird exists then his theory is false whether he finds ten white swans or ten thousand. The hallmark of a scientific theory, therefore, should be not that it has been verified (for this is impossible) but that it has withstood rigorous attempts at falsification. If a black swan were not forthcoming, then the zoologist could consider his theory corroborated for the moment. Scientific theories are thus tentative creatures that persist in the absence of conclusive evidence to the contrary.

Though the absence of disproof might be the most that science can boast, Popper argued that the record of such 'pseudo-sciences' as Marxism and Freudian psychoanalysis is a far sorrier one. Astrology, for example, makes predictions that are conveniently vague so that they cannot be proved false, whatever transpires. There is an old joke about a man investigating an international conspiracy who, when asked what he has discovered, answers: 'Nothing at all, I'm afraid – they're just too cunning.' If a theory is supposed to concern the real world, however, then it is reasonable to expect that a world in which it is correct would be different from one in which it is incorrect. If we asked the paranoid what the world would seem like if there were no international conspiracy, he would have to admit that it would appear exactly the same. His sanity is suspect not because his belief is untrue, but because the theory has no substantial content. We might even allow that what the paranoid is proposing is, in fact, true. But what exactly *is* he proposing? We might expect any conspirators to try to silence him, but if he is never attacked or bribed he may simply think they are lying low. We could tap the suspects' telephone lines to catch them trying to influence the financial markets, but if only innocent conversations turn up, the paranoid might suspect them of using other means. Either way, they must be using *some* means. And if the paranoid doubts that the investigation was carried out properly, then he will need to specify what alternative methods will be required.

Eventually we will have exhausted all the ways in which the suspects *could* be conspiring. If no hypothetical observation could ever make the paranoid change his mind, then, true or false, his theory does not seem to describe any state of affairs outside his own mind. The example shows that the less a theory admits of situations in which it might be falsified, the less it succeeds in saying about the world. This means that before any theory can be regarded as respectable, it must make predictions and risk being refuted. The fewer falsifying scenarios a theory allows for, the closer does its content shrink to vanishing point. Many commonly held views cannot be falsified, but in most cases this is no cause for worry. We cannot practically determine that there is no life outside our solar system, for example, and no matter how many barren worlds we discover, we will never be able to inspect every corner of the universe. A belief in extraterrestrials is still a meaningful one because a positive identification is possible, if unlikely. A view that cannot be falsified even in theory, however, is a view that fails to say anything about the world but often, according to Freud, has much to say about those who articulate it.

The child's theory about his toys comes dangerously close to reaching this point and failing the falsifiability test. The boy may persist in maintaining that the dolls are so clever that their movements evade every method of detection, but the toys cannot come to life without creating a possible means of their exposure. Every time they evade a new method of detection they make less of an impact on their surroundings. This process can continue until the toys become so successful in their subterfuge that they in fact fail to move at all. If belief in their movement admits no possibility of falsification, then we can ask: Of what does their movement consist? Movement that makes no sound and cannot be caught on cameras and other recording devices cannot be movement as we understand it.

The same thought offers an answer to a well-known philosophical conundrum: If a tree falls in a forest and no one hears it fall, does it make a sound? One can solve the problem simply by asking further questions. If no one saw it fall, did it make a sight? If no one felt it fall, did it make an impact? If the answer to each question is no, then pretty soon we will be left wondering how the tree actually did fall, given that falling consists of things such as loud thuds. It is as though one were trying to describe a 'duck' that had no bill, no feathers, no feet and no wings, yet was a duck all the same. If it lacks these attributes and also does not walk like a duck or quack like a duck, it is not a duck. Likewise, since we already accept that the tree fell, we must also accept that it made a sound, and a sight, and an impact.

22 | Ryle's University
When things are more than the sum
of their parts

The German philosopher and mathematician Gottfried Leibniz
(1646–1716) argued in his 1714 work, the *Monadology*, that the
human mind could not be explained in purely physical or
mechanical terms:

In imagining that there is a machine whose construction would
enable it to think, to sense, and to have perception, one could
conceive it enlarged while retaining the same proportions, so that
one could enter into it, just like into a windmill. Supposing this, one
should, when visiting within it, find only parts pushing one another,
and never anything by which to explain a perception. Thus it is in
the simple substance, and not in the composite or in the machine,
that one must look for perception.

We could similarly imagine that if a brain were to expand to
the size of Leibniz's windmill, with cells and blood vessels
acquiring the dimensions of millstones and chambers, we
would search in vain among its components and corridors for
the soul that animates us. But could it in fact be all around us
– in neither more nor less than the complexity of the structure itself? This thought was taken up by the English philosopher Gilbert Ryle in the 1940s.

Born in Brighton in 1900, Ryle was one of ten children
and the son of a doctor who was also an amateur philosopher. Unlike Leibniz, Ryle was hopeless at maths. His education was largely in the classics, though he also taught himself
Italian, German and French. Except for a period working in
Intelligence during the Second World War, Ryle spent his entire

adult life at Oxford University. In the 1920s and 1930s, a great many philosophers, especially in England, became convinced that the traditional problems of philosophy were linguistic in origin. As such, they needed to be unravelled through a rigorous analysis of grammar. As a student and lecturer at Oxford, Ryle was typical of the tweed-clad, pipe-smoking legions who sallied forth in the mid-twentieth century to expunge grammatical confusion – or metaphysics, as they said it was known. Having spent years sharpening his analytical tools, Ryle decided in the 1940s that the time had come to apply them to 'a suitable Gordian knot'. The problem he eventually settled upon was the nature of consciousness, and his thoughts on the subject were explicated in his seminal work, *The Concept of Mind*, in 1949. Reviewing the book, the philosopher J. L. Austin (1911–60) wrote, 'Not only is the book stimulating, enjoyable and original, but a quite unusually high percentage of it is true.'

Ryle identified the 'official doctrine' of consciousness, codified by René Descartes, as maintaining that every human being has a body and a mind. According to Descartes' theory, human bodies are physical objects in space, subject to the mechanical laws which govern all such objects. Minds, however, are not in space, nor are their operations subject to mechanical laws. This supposedly does not stop them from impinging upon the physical world. Through the exercise of free will, the non-physical mind can affect the body. The soul, Descartes maintained, cannot be explained in terms of our physical bodies, nor even, his successors argued, by the workings of a biochemical process inside the brain. Instead, human consciousness is the preserve of a non-physical substance that is distinct from ordinary matter. Ryle mocked this view as 'the dogma of the ghost in the machine'.

Ryle saw that Descartes' view was not fundamentally different from some of its materialist rivals. Both were reductive approaches; it was just that Descartes wished to reduce the operations of the mind to a single ethereal substance rather than a physical one. However, when we attempt to explain the mind we are not limited to invoking either ectoplasm or an undiscovered element yet to be slotted into the periodic table. To make either kind of reduction is to commit what Ryle calls a 'category mistake'. He illustrates this mistake through a number of examples. A foreigner is imagined visiting Oxford for the first time and going on a guided tour of the university. He is shown the colleges, the sports fields, the libraries and the administrative offices, but then asks, 'But where is the university? I have seen where the members of the colleges live, where the Registrar works, where the scientists experiment and the rest. But I have not yet seen the university in which reside and work the members of your university.' It then has to be explained to him that the university is not some extra component in addition to the colleges, laboratories and offices he has seen, but the way in which they are organized. The foreigner's mistake was to talk of the university as if it was in the same category or level of organization as the individual institutions he visited.

Ryle gives as another example a foreigner watching his first game of cricket. He manages to learn the functions of the bowlers, the batsmen, the fielders, the scorers and the umpire. Surprisingly, the spectator is unclear on only one thing: 'But there is no one left on the field,' he complains, 'to contribute the famous element of team spirit. I see who does the bowling, the batting and the wicket keeping; but I do not see whose role it is to exercise *esprit de corps.*' It would have to be explained to him that team spirit is not a specialized activity like batting or bowling, but the attitude with which these activities are performed. Batting enthusiastically, say, is to perform only one task rather than two. The important point is that, although exercising team spirit is not the same as simply batting or bowling, neither is it some third thing carried out separately. Similarly, to think that the mind is a non-physical thing is to make a category mistake because the mind, strictly speaking, is not a 'thing' at all. Rather, it is a phenomenon that emerges out of an organization of things.

Ryle was exposing a semantic error rather than a metaphysical one, but few people are receptive to the thought that their most cherished beliefs can be the result of getting their words in a twist. Even when we change our minds about beliefs, we do not do so on the basis of improved grammar. Grammatical errors, we normally think, are the consequences rather than the causes of mistaken beliefs. The foreign tourist of Ryle's examples could be quickly corrected by a local. But it is unlikely that a believer in the Cartesian soul could be convinced of his supposed error so easily. No Cartesian ever slapped his forehead and exclaimed 'Silly me!' on being told that he had made a category mistake. To accuse him of such an error would insult his intelligence. Nevertheless, the holistic insight employed by Ryle in his examples is indispensable.

The complexity of the mind is so divorced from its simpler components that regarding those components as spiritual rather than physical does not really help us. Far more useful is a recognition of what scientists and philosophers call 'emergence'. Emergent properties are characteristics or states that occur only when something reaches a certain level of complexity. This something might be a chemical element, a biological organism, a society or even a picture. Newspaper photographs can be seen to be made up of tiny black dots if you look closely enough. The image of President Bush, say, that emerges from those dots, is a property of their organization. It would be pointless to look for President Bush in any of the individual dots. Together they make up his portrait even though each dot is not itself a micro-president. Similarly, most neuroscientists do not go looking for consciousness in individual brain cells. There are properties belonging to consciousness and other systems that the components of brain cells do not possess on their own. Another way of saying this is that there is more to the system than the sum of its parts. The arrangement of these parts is what counts. If the organization breaks down, the emergent property would be lost: there would be no Oxford University if its colleges were disassociated from one another.

It was once tempting for scientists to imagine that there was a different substance for every kind of phenomenon. In the late seventeenth century, the German chemist and physician Johann Becher (1635–82) proposed that fire was the 'phlogiston' liberated from materials by burning. In the eighteenth century, the British chemist and physicist Joseph Black (1728–99) argued that heat was due to the 'caloric' that flowed into an object as it warmed and departed as it cooled. Other scientists tried to explain life itself by recourse to 'vital fluids'. Descartes himself believed that vital fluids moved the body hydraulically. The heat of a flame would displace the skin of the hand, which in turn would tug on a thread that went all the way up to the pineal gland in the brain. A valve would then open which would release vital fluids down a pipe to inflate the muscles of the arm and move your hand away from the flame. Few scientists today believe that substances such as vital fluids exist, as the phenomena they attempt to explain can be accounted for without their help – through the effects of natural processes involving atoms and molecules and neurones and receptors.

If we accept that consciousness is an emergent property of brains, we face another problem that Descartes was trying to avoid with his dualistic theory. That is, if the mind is ultimately reliant for its existence on ordinary physical matter, then it would seem to be incapable of exerting free will. This is because, it is argued, cause and effect work on the microscopic level and not on the macroscopic level where consciousness emerges. If a holistic state – such as a photograph of President Bush – causes you to remember one of his speeches, this is only because the atoms in the surface of the photograph bounce photons of light on to your retina, which then send a certain combination of nerve impulses around your brain. The laws of physics do not recognize organized states such as pictures. They work only in units such as atoms and photons. The universe itself, we might say, is not aware that certain vibrations of air molecules are President Bush's words of wisdom, or even that President Bush exists. The thought is that causation works from the bottom up. That is to say that events on the microscopic level can have knock-on effects further up the scale of organization, but events further up that scale cannot cause anything to happen on the lower level. This is not to disparage the president's powers of rhetoric, merely to point out that his words only cause something to happen by virtue of their simpler physical properties. Any causation must work in terms of atoms and the like and, if that is so, then the fact that certain arrangements of atoms constitute conscious-ness is by the by. Philosophers call such states 'epiphenomenal', meaning that they can be caused but cannot themselves cause anything in turn. This is a curious form of powerlessness akin to someone who is buffeted by events around him yet cannot himself make the slightest difference to his circumstances. Condemned in this way, emergent states such as consciousness do not really fulfil the important roles we ascribe to them, such as executing choices. Instead, the mind is like an audience that cannot participate in the show (its own show, in fact). In the terms of Ryle's analogy, the activities of Oxford's individual colleges can affect the standing of the university as a whole, but the standing of the university is not the sort of thing that can then turn round and affect the activities of the colleges.

This view is another variant of the substance reductionism Ryle wanted to abolish. Instead of resorting to souls or lumpen matter, we now have a more arcane form of matter to which everything – consciousness included – is to be reduced. This third substance is very different to matter as we know it in the form of bodies and boulders. It is different even from atoms, since atoms themselves can be divided into subatomic particles.

This substance is in fact mythical. The ghost in the machine may have been exorcized, but we now have a veritable ghost in the atom. According to quantum theory, there are no particles at all, let alone ones to which everything more complex can be reduced. What seem to be particles are supposedly better described, physicists tell us, as patterns of excitation in quantum fields. These fields and their activities seem to be irreducibly pattern-like, in that there is nothing more to them than their arrangements: their very existence consists in their configurations.

This does not mean, however, that every property we might regard as emergent warrants the description. In the nineteenth century, when the philosopher John Stuart Mill was discussing emergence he identified chemical reactions as processes that were more than the sum of each reactant. Today, we have a better understanding of chemistry and can explain reactions entirely in terms of the movement of electrons from one atom to another. We cannot know whether the same fate will not some day befall the notion of mental states as emergent phenomena. What we can tell, though, is that this need not matter greatly. In the event, we may not have to revise the way we talk, or even philosophize, about things such as emotions and free will. Take, for example, the question of why we enjoy music. One suggestion is that abstract sounds may resemble the cadences of our mother's voice that we remember from infancy. Another is that the movement in a rhythm is analogous to the movement of our bodies when engaged in exciting activities such as sex or hunting. Or it may be that music reminds us of heaven, where it was constantly played while we were waiting in the celestial antechamber prior to birth. As far as they go, all these theories describe our appreciation of music as an emergent property that depends upon a certain level of organization. According to both the reductive materialist and the neo-Cartesian, they are all nonsense. The materialist would say that musical appreciation is a certain brain state caused by certain vibrations in air molecules. The believer in souls, meanwhile, would make a similar point in terms of his own ethereal substances.

The question, then, is what do these two think we are talking about in the first place? The pleasure we experience when we listen to a symphony may be caused by vibrations in the air, but this does not mean that those vibrations are not at the same time a symphony. Explanations at the level of symphonies will be equally as valid for their own purposes. Conversely, if the pleasure they cause is truly reducible to a neural pattern in the brain, it would not be right to say that pleasure is epiphenomenal in a way that the brain pattern is not. If emotions and certain neural patterns are in fact one and the same, then fear, anger and desire will be perfectly capable of causing us to act. In turn, the choices we freely make in response to these emotions will be equally effective if they are identical with the firing of neurones that moves our limbs. Ironically, it transpires that protecting the integrity of our emotions by identifying them as emergent properties was exactly what led to them being deemed epiphenomenal, capable of being acted upon but not of exerting influence themselves. Reductive materialism has long been thought a threat to the powers and significance of conscious feeling and thought, but once the mind is reduced to its constituents it takes on all their causal powers. If only we would take the materialist reductionist shilling, we could have our free will back.

In the final reckoning there may be no such thing as a truly emergent property, one that can never be read off from its components. Emergence would then be a quality we attribute merely to phenomena that we do not yet understand. But until then, emergence is why we need chemistry, biology and psychology instead of just physics to understand life.

23 | Turing's Machine
Computing the unthinkable

During a sermon by his school chaplain, the British newspaper columnist Miles Kington was once asked to imagine the following tale. During the Second World War, Germany's air defences begin to exact a potentially ruinous toll on the Royal Air Force's bomber crews. Bomber Command hits upon the bright idea of towing decoy bombers behind the real aircraft. These decoys are plywood shells, but in the night sky they are easily mistaken for Lancasters and help to draw flak from the real bombers. The ploy works until German gunners learn to distinguish the decoys from the Lancasters by their outlines. In response, more convincing decoys are constructed which, from the outside, look just like the real thing. Again, the plan works until the Germans devise a means of picking out the real bombers from the heat signature of their engines. The decoys then have to be fitted with engines. It is not long before these too are rumbled, as radio operators on the ground can tell that the decoys are not sending or receiving transmissions. Eventually, the RAF is forced to make its decoys perfect and at this point realizes that they might as well carry bombs and join in the fighting. The final decoys are so realistic that they are in fact not decoys at all, but real Lancaster bombers.

A philosopher might say that if one thing mimics another perfectly, then it indeed becomes that thing. The man in the street would put it differently: if it walks like a duck and quacks like a duck, it is a duck. The thought behind this is that function is definitive – a thing is defined by what it does, or what it is capable of doing. While philosophers and laymen alike are happy to apply this tool to ducks, they often recoil from analysing human beings in this way. Humans are not just what they do – they also have internal lives. People may walk and talk, but so, in theory, can zombies or automatons. What separates us from these simulacra is that we possess conscious minds. But perhaps we are not doing our rivals justice. What if we were presented not with the hopelessly unconvincing ghouls and lumbering robots of B-movie science fiction, but with creatures that were to all intents and purposes indistinguishable from real people? This was the question to which the computer scientist Alan Turing proposed an interesting answer.

Turing was born in London in 1912, the son of an imperial administrator in India. He grew up with his older brother in various foster homes in England while his parents remained abroad. His interest in science apparently began when he was given a book titled *Natural Wonders Every Child Should Know*. He seems to have received little else in the way of encouragement, especially from his mother, who worried that his scientific bent would be frowned upon by an English public school. Her fears were confirmed when the headmaster at Sherborne School duly reported that her son was 'wasting his time' there. Turing nevertheless found an intellectual companion at Sherborne in Christopher Morcom, a boy one year above him. Morcom's premature death from tuberculosis in 1930 deprived Turing of this companionship, but it seems that it also planted in him a philosophical curiosity concerning the human mind and whether that of his friend could have survived the death of his body. Turing sought the answer in physics and mathematics rather than philosophical speculation.

At Cambridge University, Turing set about investigating the essence of calculation. He reasoned that it was a relatively mindless thought process, one that could be carried out by a machine following certain rules just as well as, or better than, a human being. For example, a machine could be devised that could calculate the factors of a given number. Another could be designed to enact the rules of chess. Turing realized that it was not necessary to have different machines to follow each set of rules. He imagined a 'universal' machine consisting of a head under which a tape was passed bearing a binary series of zeros and ones. The head could read and write these digits and move to other points on the tape according to the rules of its program. Given enough time and a sufficiently long tape, the machine could, in theory, calculate the answer to any problem expressible in binary code. If this machine could not solve a given problem, then that problem would be impossible to solve by any machine following the mechanical rules of logic. The universal machine was the theoretical forerunner of today's computers.

Turing's research was of great help to the Allied cause during the Second World War. The coded transmissions sent by the German armed forces were scrambled using the fabled Enigma machines. These devices looked like humble typewriters, but could encode a message typed into them in German with a cipher that was deemed unbreakable. At the secret code-breaking centre at Bletchley Park in 1943, Turing and his colleagues built Colossus, the only machine that could defeat Enigma. Colossus was composed of valves and vacuum tubes rather than the electronic circuits of today's microprocessors, yet it worked in binary digits and could scan 25,000 characters of a coded message for regularities in one second and find a key. The machine was refined until it took only a matter of minutes to decode a communiqué. At a time when the loss of shipping meant that Britain might be starved out of the war, the cracking of the Enigma code enabled the Allies to track every German U-boat in the Atlantic Ocean.

There are few individuals who could be said to have made as significant a contribution to the Allied victory as Alan Turing. Yet while Nazi war criminals remained free in South America, the creator of Colossus was persecuted at home. In 1952 he was arrested for conducting a homosexual relationship with a young man from Manchester. He did not attempt to deny it, but instead argued that there was nothing wrong with his actions. He was tried and found guilty and, in lieu of a year's imprisonment, submitted to a course of oestrogen injections designed to reduce the libido of sexual 'deviants'. As known homosexuals were ineligible for security clearance, he was also forced to give up his code-breaking work for the government. Despite his defiant front, Turing was found dead from cyanide poisoning two years later. His mother believed that it was an accident, that the half-eaten apple beside his bed showed that the poison had remained on his fingers from a chemistry experiment. This may have been what he wanted her to believe, for the coroner's verdict was suicide. Turing's legacy, and that of Bletchley Park, was the worldwide computer revolution of the late twentieth century.

The descendants of Colossus, Turing believed, would one day possess minds in the same way that human beings do. If a machine were sophisticated enough and programmed with the correct rules, it could reproduce the processes of human thought through brute force of calculation. Turing thought it worked the other way round too: 'A man provided with paper, pencil, and rubber, and subject to strict discipline, is,' he said, 'in effect a universal machine.' There was no difference, he maintained, between the processes of thought and the nature of thought itself. The point is that to think is to calculate, in one way or another. Turing devised a simple test for consciousness – now known as the Turing test – by which he thought we could settle the matter, should so sophisticated a machine be produced. Many variants of the Turing test have been proposed, but they all rely on a computer being able to convince a human being that it is in fact another human. A human being and a computer are placed in different rooms and someone is allowed to question them both without coming face to face with them. Let's assume that they communicate via email rather than by telephone, or otherwise the computer's synthetic accent might give it away at once. If the interrogator cannot tell which one is the human being, then the machine has passed the Turing test and possesses a mind. 'By the end of the century,' Turing wrote, 'the use of words and general educated opinion will have altered so much that one will be able to speak of machines thinking without expecting to be contradicted.' We are now in the twenty-first century, and no machine has even come close to passing the Turing test on a regular basis. Computers may have beaten the world's greatest chess player, but the victorious Deep Blue program remains incapable of holding a simple conversation with an adult human being. However, this does not mean that no machine will *ever* pass the test.

The issue is whether a machine would be conscious even if it did pass the Turing test. Turing himself wrote: 'The original question "Can machines think?" I believe to be too meaningless to deserve discussion.' At Cambridge University, he had attended Ludwig Wittgenstein's seminars. Though these meetings had concentrated on the philosophy of mathematics, it was the Austrian philosopher's view that the supposedly private, internal life of the mind stands in need of outward criteria. That is to say that if its qualities could not be expressed publicly, we could not talk meaningfully of the mind at all. In this case, the criteria for conscious thought laid down in the Turing test would be not only sufficient, but the very things of which consciousness actually consists: intelligent linguistic behaviour. So once the test was passed by a machine, no further discussion would be necessary. In everyday life, we believe our fellows to be conscious and not simply automatons because they are constantly passing the Turing test. If we were to observe their actions and their speech and then ask, 'But are they *conscious*?' we would have no further criteria by which this question could be settled. It is simply part of the rules of our language and understanding that intelligent behaviour and speech equate with consciousness.

This argument denies that there is a difference between appearance and reality when it comes to language use. There does seem to be a difference, however, in the American philosopher John Searle's story of the Chinese room. Searle (1932–) imagined a room and a man sitting in it who does not understand a single word of Chinese. Through a letterbox, the man receives questions written in Chinese characters and responds by looking them up in tables and passing back the symbols indicated by the tables to be the appropriate answer. In essence, this is what a computer that apparently 'understood' Chinese would do. By that rationale, since the man in the room does not understand Chinese, neither does the computer. The point is that both are functioning merely as mindless manipulators of symbols.

It may be that Searle is looking for understanding in the wrong place. The man in the room may not understand Chinese, but perhaps the man *and* the tables within the room taken as a system do. It is the whole room that should be regarded as the language user if there is to be an accurate analogy of a symbol-processing computer. Just as we do not locate understanding in a special part of a Chinese speaker's brain, we cannot expect understanding to reside in the computer's CPU. Though the whole, whether person or machine, may understand Chinese, any particular part of it might not. Searle's rejoinder is to imagine that the man in the room has memorized the tables. The entire system would then be internalized – and he still would not understand Chinese.

Many people seem to speak their second or third languages like this. Where a Chinese child speaks his language fluently, others coming to Chinese late in life might have to think in their first language while they construct Chinese sentences in their heads before speaking them. Despite their difficulties, it would be unfair to say that they do not understand the language at all. But they possess something that the man in the Chinese room lacks; namely, a knowledge of the things in the world to which the Chinese characters refer. Far from undermining Searle's argument, the isolation of the Chinese room actually reinforces it. It shows that cognition is more than the manipulation of pure symbols of which Turing machines are capable. However, this does not mean that computers will never be able to think, merely that in order to do so they would have to operate in a certain way so that the symbols they manipulate become meaningful to them. It would not be a simple case of programming a computer with the rules for language. Rather, the computer would also have to learn about the world through a means analogous to our own. This takes the debate outside the boundaries of the Turing test, for a machine could pass it without meeting this requirement. This does not compromise the integrity of the tool that was used to construct the test, as long as we remember that what something can be said to do is influenced by how it came to be doing it. Should a machine ever pass the Turing test and also withstand a critical examination of its educational history, it would seem churlish to deny that it had a mind. To remain intransigent would perhaps betray a prejudice against silicon similar to the one which advocates of the soul once held against the flesh.

24 | Dawkins's Meme
How ideas think of us

When Copernicus placed the sun at the centre of the solar system in 1530, it began to dawn on human beings that the universe might not have been created solely for our benefit. When Charles Darwin published *The Origin of Species* in 1859, we were forced to accept that man might not have been given dominion over the natural world as his birthright. In 1953, Francis Crick's and James Watson's discovery of DNA implied that even our bodies were not designed with our own interests in mind, but rather those of our genes. In *The Selfish Gene* (1976), Richard Dawkins, the evolutionary biologist who has done so much to promote this conclusion, added the final insult: not even the contents of our own minds are designed for our benefit. Rather than looking merely at how and why we develop and communicate ideas, Dawkins suggested that ideas can propagate themselves under their own steam according to Darwinian principles.

Dawkins is now Professor of the Public Understanding of Science at Oxford University. He was born in 1941 in Kenya, where his father was stationed during the Second World War. The family returned to England when he was nine years old. In 1959, he went to Oxford to study zoology. Earlier in that decade, Crick and Watson had discovered the double helix structure of DNA, and microbiologists began to take over from zoologists and naturalists in producing descriptions of nature. Dawkins transformed himself from a zoologist into an evolutionary biologist, but he brought with him the zoologist's tools of studying cooperative and competitive behaviour and applied them to the subjects of microbiology: genes. In a series of lucid books beginning with *The Selfish Gene*, Dawkins charted the natural history of what he has called 'the river out of Eden' – the flow of information passing down the ages in the genomes of living things.

Dawkins championed the ideas of George Williams and Robert Travers in the US and William Hamilton and John Maynard Smith in the UK. These scientists developed the view that the forces of natural selection – whereupon those features best adapted to their environment are the ones that survive and proliferate in the ecosystem – operate not upon species, or even individuals within a species, but at the level of the gene. The reasoning was as follows. Imagine that a species were to conduct itself in order to further the interests of every one of its members, say, by amassing a shared store of food to get everyone through the winter. It would be in the interests of an individual of that species to break the pact and gobble up as much of that food as it could while leaving everyone else to do the gathering. Human beings may have idiosyncratic notions of cooperation and the common good which tell them not to act in this way, even if their altruism is often merely enlightened self-interest or the fear of punishment. But these sentiments are not available to simpler creatures, whose self-interest does not have the sophistication to become 'enlightened'. A species, as a unit, is unable to act in the common interest *en masse* because this aim will run up against the contrary interests of its selfish individual members. It is not that individual germs or worms or ants are incapable of acting selflessly, merely that any members of the species who do will soon find themselves dying off, leaving the selfish ones to enjoy their good fortune.

This analysis is repeated on the level of the individual. There are innumerable instances in nature of creatures acting against the interests of their own survival, such as when skylarks sacrifice their own safety for that of their young. Whose self-interest is at work here? It cannot be that of baby skylarks – who do not, as far as we know, threaten their mother into leaving the nest to decoy predators. And it clearly cannot be that of the mother, who receives nothing from her young in return and sometimes ends up in the jaws of a hungry wolf for her trouble. Dawkins argues that she is in fact acting in the interests of her genes, which are also present in the bodies of her young and which will be more likely to survive and reproduce themselves in future generations of skylarks if she sacrifices herself. It is significant that this process is entirely mindless. It is not that her genes are urging her on or 'want' her to act in this way – for they do not even know that she exists – simply that the genes which can affect the behaviour of their 'hosts' stand a better chance of surviving and replicating themselves throughout the world than those which constitute selfish skylarks that fly off and allow their broods to be devoured by predators. If there were smaller replicating units which made up genes themselves, then the self-interest of those units would no doubt get to have their say before genes. Since genes are the most basic unit of replication, however, the buck stops with them. Strictly speaking, genes are not capable of functioning in their own interest or those of other genes, they simply function as they do, and the ones that function selfishly, in terms of furthering their replication in the most possible instances, are the ones that proliferate.

Humans, for their part, are not quite in the grip of their genes in this way. As Dawkins remarks, we frustrate the interests of our genes every time we use contraception. Human minds, with their attendant wills and whims, can do pretty much as they please. Indeed, we are on the verge of the ability now, despite our fears over 'designer babies' and the spectre of eugenics, to alter directly the structure of our DNA through genetic engineering. Dawkins had the further thought, however, that what he realized to be true of genes might also follow for any kind of thing that was capable of replicating itself. Ideas too have this property of replicability. You find yourself humming a tune and then remember that you heard it five minutes ago on the radio, then later, after you have stopped, you notice that your colleague has begun to hum the same tune. If it is a particularly catchy tune you may find yourself humming it again and again, each time passing on what Dawkins calls this 'meme' to more and more people.

All kinds of ideas, fashions, catchphrases and skills are infectious. The philosophical tools presented in this book – memes included – can be thought of as memes in this way. As human beings, we seem to have a propensity to copy others. It is in copying the thoughts and hearsay of others that we make our first steps in education. We also feel it wise to copy the ideas and mannerisms of the most successful among us, whether they be the fashions worn by Princess Diana or *The Seven Habits of Highly Effective People* in business. Mimicry may be so important to survival that we cannot help but find ourselves indulging in it. Dawkins argues that memes are in fact as essential a part of our evolutionary make-up as genes themselves. We have survived as the fittest so far not just because of the hardy bodies and opposable thumbs with which our genes furnish us, but also because our memes enable us to manipulate our environment with tools and skills. Just as bees build hives and birds build nests, humans construct artefacts to further their survival. Where we differ from the birds and the bees here is that our own artefacts are not built into our genetic make-up. Birds apparently do not have to learn how to build a nest, but the ability to manufacture automobiles is not something humans are born with. While the human genome evolves through the aeons, memes pursue their own evolution as they are passed on and adapt through the generations. Some memes, like some organisms, reproduce at a prodigious rate but do not live for very long while others take a long time to develop but then hang around for millennia. An example of the first kind would be a fashion for wearing a certain colour that changes with the seasons. Instances of the second kind are more controversial, the striking examples of which are religious movements.

What, on further thought, can seem quite chilling about memes is that though we may worry about our ideas, ideas themselves have only one purpose: to replicate themselves. They are every bit as selfish as the selfish gene, and Dawkins uses strong language to describe their operation. He talks of memes 'infecting' our minds 'like viruses'. When I hear someone whistle a catchy tune, it 'parasitizes' my brain and then propagates in the brains of others, just as a virus parasitizes the cells of an organism in order to make further copies of itself. And like, say, the genes that cause cancer, memes that are good at propagating themselves may not always be good for the host. For the sake of argument, thousands of people in the Middle Ages were infected with the thought that if they punished themselves through regular self-flagellation and fasting, then God would not feel moved to punish them with the Plague. Their efforts did nothing but lower their resistance to the disease that killed many of them. Equally futile was the anti-Semitic tradition in Europe that led not only to the murder of approximately six million Jews in the Holocaust but also to the death of its foremost proponents by the end of the Second World War. Some memes may be so bad for us that they destroy their own means of propagation. For obvious reasons, the idea that jumping off cliffs is a good thing is never going to enjoy ubiquity in the meme pool.

On the other hand, memes such as the ability to drive a car or count to ten are beneficial in a similar way to genes that lead to sharp eyesight or strong legs for sprinting. Since we have limited time in which to consider ideas, and because some doctrines are mutually exclusive, all memes must compete for our attention. Among the varied ways in which they do this is by being useful to us, and by helping us to survive or prosper in particular circumstances. By this criterion, it is no wonder that inventions such as fire, warm clothing and the cure for smallpox have enjoyed such a happy marriage with human minds. But as far as the memes are concerned, the advantage they bestow on their possessors is mere coincidence. If that advantage means that more minds will be receptive to them, then that is well and good, but the first priority is to infect as many minds as possible whatever the consequences may be. To achieve this, memes need to persuade people to promulgate them, and bestowing survival advantages is only one way of going about this. Another way is to be very difficult to shift once they have been accepted. One such meme, Dawkins argues, is religious faith. Bolstered by the obloquy heaped upon Doubting Thomas, the faith meme disables the critical faculties that might otherwise question and expunge it. Other examples include conspiracy theory memes, which carry with them the defence that the less evidence there is for the conspiracy, the more powerful and cunning the conspirators must be. Belief in UFOs too can be attributed to an errant meme, one that was invented in the United States in the 1940s and has been proliferating ever since. Some memes take such a hold of us that they rearrange our minds, making them more receptive to other similar memes. What start out as notions then become attitudes. Feelings of paranoia seem to work in this way. Once we begin to imagine that our partner is having an affair, we can start to interpret everything they do as secretive. We then ask why they should want to have an affair, and begin to question other things about ourselves too. Dawkins identifies these memes as mental viruses that take over the mind of their host much as a computer virus might take over the operating system of a PC. In the case of religion, he has argued that they get into our mental bloodstream when our defences are low – when we are young and gullible children.

It is because of this view that Dawkins is as famed for his atheism as he is for his biological theories. Reasonably enough, the religious-minded have not taken kindly to the suggestion that they are suffering from a kind of mental illness. They maintain, for instance, that religious views are not without their uses. These might make us happier or more optimistic about life, and they have certainly inspired a canon of great art and a history of civic progress. However, this does not mean that they are true. What it does show is that those memes proliferate which are useful not primarily for our biological survival – since tithing to the Church leaves us less income to spend on food and shelter – but for the things that we hold to be important, whatever they may be. It is not only religious memes that work on this basis. From pastimes such as rock climbing to revolutionary politics, we serve the interests of our feelings and ideas as enthusiastically as we seek self-preservation. In the last century, ideological memes led us to stockpile enough nuclear weaponry to destroy the entire world several times over. Just like genes, memes are well or badly adapted according to the environment in which they find themselves. And if that environment is a crazy one, there will always be plenty of memes that are perfectly at home in it. That said, whether a habitat is 'sane' or not may depend largely upon which memes have constructed the cultural background.

The terms of this debate have created an artificial distinction between 'them' and 'us'. When we ask who is in charge, us or our memes, we have to remember that we may want to bring certain memes within the boundaries of the self rather than regarding them as outside influences. The procedures of rational thought that enable us to differentiate between good and bad memes are themselves memes, yet we would not think of them as aliens that have somehow managed to infect our minds. Such memes have perhaps been so successful in establishing themselves that they stand in a similar relation to us as the energy-producing mitochondria that invaded the cells of our ancestors billions of years ago and without which we would die. Certain memes, such as notions of right and wrong or truth and falsehood, are not just an optional extra for our mental life, but are part of what makes us human.

Despite its early insights, memetics has not so far proved to be a fertile field of thought. Most of the books (and even more of the websites) devoted to memes are disappointingly full of nothing but hot air. Much of the literature on the subject, digital and printed, has been produced by a fringe of self-proclaimed philosophers and those professionals who only wish to add to their own particular hotchpotch of post-modern verbiage. But the weakness of memetics as a science is not due solely to the shortcomings of many of its practitioners. The comparison of memes with genes is largely an analogy and not one that holds perfectly. Memes can blend with each other whereas genes are particulate and cannot. Memes can also adapt to their environment within the lifetime of their host and then be passed on to his or her progeny with their modifications intact. Genes, on the other hand, cannot be transformed by the activities of their host, they merely survive into the next generation or fail to do so. Most importantly, before the advent of genetic engineering, new genes could only arise through chance mutation. Though some memes are created in this way, through a 'bolt of inspiration' as it were, many others are consciously designed through the hard work of purposive thinking and reasoning.

Long before we devised genetic engineering, we developed the ability to directly alter our received ideas and instincts. Memetic engineering, or rational thought as it is commonly known, gives us power over memes. In the mental sphere as opposed to the physical, we learned to manipulate the units of replication before we knew why we had them. But as the victims of war and ideological persecution can unfortunately tell us, like genetic engineering, this manipulation remains somewhat unreliable.

25 | Derrida and Deconstruction
Taking ideas apart

In 1938, the American illustrator Bob Kane created Batman, the famous comic-book character who fights crime on the streets of Gotham City. Unlike the equally popular Superman with his array of supernatural powers, Batman dispatched his enemies with nothing more than unarmed combat and a utility belt. The most pointed difference between the two characters, however, was the latter's motivation. Whereas the Man of Steel was concerned primarily with truth, justice and the American way, Batman embarked on his crime-fighting career after his parents were murdered by a mugger. He was after revenge. This quality was brought out by Frank Miller in 1986 in *The Dark Knight Returns*, which depicted Batman as a brutal vigilante and as psychologically twisted as those he fights. To use the terminology of the French philosopher Jacques Derrida, Batman 'deconstructs' the concept of the hero. The story demonstrates how a concept we regard as clear and fixed is in fact enmeshed with its antithesis. It is not only that adversity or villainy are required to provide an opportunity for heroism, but that these qualities are entangled in the very act of heroism – as when Batman uses violence to defeat his nemesis, the Joker. Deconstruction, broadly speaking, is the way in which we bring to light the contradictions hidden in our familiar beliefs and concepts. Without the Joker, Batman would not be a superhero but merely a man in a ridiculous outfit.

Jacques Derrida was born in 1930 in Algiers to a lower-middle-class Jewish family. After the fall of France in 1940, the Nazi persecution of Jews was instigated in French Algeria despite the absence of any German occupier. Jewish children were segregated into special schools and teachers lost their jobs without much in the way of protest from their colleagues. Even after liberation by the Allies, racial laws were maintained for a further six months by the supposedly 'free' French government. For one whole year, Derrida saw no reason to turn up for lessons. He dreamed of becoming a soccer player but after finding that he could not play well enough he moved to France to study when he was nineteen. After being admitted to the Ecole Normal Supérieure in Paris in 1952, Derrida joined a number of far-left political groups and enrolled in philosophy classes as a result of hearing a radio programme about his fellow countryman, the writer Albert Camus (1913–60). Though Derrida has a chequered history of examinations – failing first his baccalaureate in 1947, later the entrance examination to the Ecole Normal Supérieure twice and finally the first attempt at his teaching qualification – he has since taught philosophy at the Sorbonne in Paris and at Yale University in the United States. Derrida has campaigned for such causes as the end of apartheid in South Africa and freedom of expression in Czechoslovakia prior to the election of Václav Havel as president in 1989. In 1982, he travelled to Czechoslovakia where, though he merely participated in an 'unofficial' seminar conducted by dissidents and visited Kafka's grave, the authorities saw fit to arrest him on scurrilous charges of drugs possession.

More controversy has surrounded Derrida's philosophical views than his political beliefs, however. He received widespread coverage in the British press, for example, when several senior members of Cambridge University opposed awarding him an honorary degree in 1992. The award was put to the vote, and though the result was 336–204 in Derrida's favour, it was the first time in twenty-nine years that a ballot had been necessary. The split demonstrated the suspicion with which the Anglo-American and Continental traditions in philosophy continue to regard one another. In the face of accusations of charlatanry and obscurantism, Derrida remains cheerful and refuses to take this criticism too seriously. In an interview with *Le Nouvel Observateur* in 1983, he declared that he did not seek difficulty for its own sake. He claimed, on the contrary, that those who profess to find his work unintelligible often understand it very well: 'No one gets angry with a mathematician or with a doctor he doesn't understand at all,' he complained, 'or with someone who speaks a foreign language . . . Why is it that we seem to ask the philosopher to be "easy" and not other such scholars who are even more inaccessible to the very same readers?' However, it is not only the layman who asks Derrida to make sense – it is often professional philosophers who have spent decades studying their subject and suspect his impenetrable prose style to mask a lack of rigour or depth of argument. The British doctor and philosopher Raymond Tallis once remarked, 'When the emperor is restocking his wardrobe he usually shops in Paris.'

Derrida's work is certainly obscure, and he resists any canonical formulation of his views. This is because he does not believe that meanings can be grasped 'all at once' by means of a handy concept. In this case, no definition of deconstruction could suffice. In a letter to Professor Izutsu in Japan dated 10 July 1983, he wrote:

Deconstruction is not a method and cannot be transformed into one . . . It is true that in certain circles (university or cultural, especially in the United States) the technical and methodological 'metaphor' that seems necessarily attached to the very word 'deconstruction' has been able to seduce or lead astray . . . It is not enough to say that deconstruction could not be reduced to some methodological instrumentality or to a set of rules and transposable procedures. Nor will it do to claim that each deconstructive 'event' remains singular or, in any case, as close as possible to something like an idiom or a signature. It must also be made clear that deconstruction is not even an *act* or an *operation*.

Having ruled out these approaches, Derrida goes on to say that 'the word "deconstruction" like all other words acquires its value only from its inscription in a chain of possible substitutions, in what is [too] blithely called a "context"'. We need to see the procedure in action in order to understand it.

Derrida illustrates deconstruction with an example from the history of philosophy in *Dissemination* (1972). In the *Phaedrus*, Plato tells the myth of Thoth and Thamus – the god who invented writing and the Egyptian king to whom Thoth offered his creation. Thamus refuses the gift, judging that its dangers outweigh its benefits for mankind. On the one hand, writing offers a new form of cultural memory that can store far more information than is handed down from generation to generation via the oral tradition. However, if people no longer have to go about the difficult business of learning things by heart since they can now look them up at will in books, their powers of memory are bound to fall into decline. Books also do away with the guiding presence of a teacher, and without such a custodian of learning the pupil might misinterpret what he reads. Thamus is also concerned that the social bonds of paternal sanction and filial obligation will be dissolved. These ties ensure it is true knowledge that is handed down from master to pupil – for the mature and wise teacher has greater authority than paper and ink. Where a human teacher can bring knowledge to life in the minds of individuals, writing imparts merely a kind of rote-learning, a mechanical device for producing a simulacrum of knowledge. Even today we in the West often sneer at those who learned everything they know from books, as if this somehow discounts their knowledge or means that they do not really understand it. Derrida argues that the privileging of speech over writing is a prejudice endemic in the Western tradition of philosophy and religion.

Derrida notices that whenever Plato comes to talk of 'good' uses of language and memory in the *Phaedrus*, he falls back on metaphors derived from the practice of writing. The things given positive value in the story – such as speech, living memory and the presence of the teacher – are defined in contrast to that which threatens them. Speech, for example, is not held up as something entirely different from writing, but as a 'good' kind of writing – that which is 'written in the soul of the learner'. Information stored in the memories of individuals rather than texts is similarly described with metaphors of engraving and inscription. This use of simile may be thought subsidiary to the main thrust of the text, or as superfluous to its meaning. Plato could have used different metaphors, or no metaphors at all, but Derrida argues that they must be taken into account in an adequate reading of the text.

According to the definition of writing used by thinkers from Plato to the Swiss linguist Ferdinand de Saussure (1857–1913), writing operates at two removes from the truth. By speaking, we produce signs for what we mean. Writing in turn manufactures further signs, in the form of phonetically transcribed words for these signs. Derrida's point is that all expression shares the predicament of writing, because expression always comes too late in the process of communication to be a reliable carrier of sense. According to the traditional account, metaphor is a deviation from the normal procedure in which words literally mean what they are intended to. But how, Derrida asks, could words acquire this fantastic ability to latch on to what they express? He is not the only thinker to deny that meaning consists in an ideal correspondence between the sound of a spoken word and the sense it is supposed to be expressing. The relationship is an arbitrary one, and one that may be subject to change over time. A deconstructive approach pays scrupulous regard to the letter of texts so that it can expose supposedly literal meanings as being disguised metaphors.

Deconstruction attempts to show that words and concepts do not deliver what they promise. In the discussion of games in section 66 of *Philosophical Investigations*, Ludwig Wittgenstein illustrates presciently how gaps always appear when we try to explain a concept:

Look for example at board games, with their multifarious relationships. Now pass to card games; here you may find many correspondences with the first group, but many common features drop out, and others appear. When we pass next to ball games, much that is common is retained, but much is lost. – Are they all 'amusing'? Compare chess with noughts and crosses. Or is there always winning and losing, or competition between players? Think of patience. In ball games there is winning and losing; but when a child throws his ball at the wall and catches it again, this feature has disappeared. Look at the parts played by skill and luck; and at the difference between skill in chess and skill in tennis. Think now of games like ring-a-ring-a-roses; here is the element of amusement, but how many other characteristic features have disappeared! And we can go through the many, many other groups of games in the same way; can see how similarities crop up and disappear.

The ways in which we can describe a concept are potentially endless, and every account we give will omit or exclude others. The object of deconstruction is not to show how such gaps can be filled to make our description more complete and accurate, but to show that gaps are unavoidable. It does this not by appealing to a criterion of completeness that lies outside our texts and speeches, but by examining in detail their implications. Suppose I decide that my fiancée is 'the perfect woman'. If I am besotted then I must deem her perfect, yet my concept of perfection cannot be perfect. This imperfect concept is the only one I possess, however, so at the same time there will always be a sense in which my fiancée is *not* 'the perfect woman'.

According to Derrida, we can never arrive at definitive accounts of our concepts. His point does not just hold for philosophical ideas. When we analyse even a mundane event in great detail, it seems to disappear, leaving its inputs and outputs. For example, when a fire breaks out, we talk of its causes and effects, imagining that the 'fire' occurred somewhere between these two. But after we have enumerated the 'before' and 'after' we find that these phases meet in the middle, leaving no time for the 'event'. This event could not be the striking of a match, for that too comprises a series of events that can be divided into 'before' and 'after'. Similarly, a half-familiar word can seem pregnant with meaning, but when we look it up in a dictionary it becomes a husk, its meaning 'squeezed out' into that of its synonyms.

However, these observations do not seem to interfere with our ability to communicate with each other. If I tell the fire brigade that my house is on fire, they will know what to expect when they arrive, and my insurance company will understand what I mean when I claim that the blaze broke out in my kitchen at around six o'clock. This is because ordinary language does not require the precision demanded by deconstruction. If I say that an apple is red, I am not contradicted by finding green specks upon its skin. My description may be 'incomplete', but we are entitled to ask where Derrida's fascination with completeness comes from. Indeed, to add more and more detail often works against clarity, as when background noise in a recording studio spoils the work of a sound engineer. Much communication relies precisely on what we say being incomplete. But even then it is incomplete only from the point of view of a description of *everything*. If I am looking for a pattern, I want only a complete description of the pattern – not necessarily one of the pattern *plus* its surroundings. There is only a problem, then, if things cannot ever be separated from their surroundings, and this is what Derrida maintains. He subscribes to the view that meaning is a product of context – that a sign means something by virtue of its place within a whole system of signs. Furthermore, he argues that the context is a shifting one, that language is a torrent that moves too fast for us to fix meanings to terms in isolation for the purpose of exegesis. Language possesses 'iterability' – that is, a piece of speech can be reproduced in a different context and still possess a meaning. According to Derrida's thought, it is precisely this ability to travel that prohibits statements from possessing a determinate meaning that a listener or reader can know for sure. However, while the iterability of our concepts guarantees that they will be incomplete, without it no one would be able to understand anything that anyone said except the speaker himself.

The value in Derrida's work lies in getting us to see the traces of what has been omitted from our concepts and descriptions, for these lacunae are part of what makes them possible. The notion of brotherhood, for example, implies that there can be people who are not my brothers to which my fellowship will not apply. (A club to which *everyone* has membership is not a club.) In order to include my brothers under this concept, there must be others who are excluded. When we realize this, we are given an opportunity to make a moral decision: whether to retain our concept or exchange it. As Derrida says, 'We have to study the models and the history of the models and then try not to subvert them for the sake of destroying them but to change the models and invent new ways of writing – not as a formal challenge, but for ethical, political reasons.' Deconstruction prompts us to rethink the basis of our practices, concepts and values. We might carry on as before, or we might look for new values and identities instead. As we look at what was left out (and consider how to include it), however, we will need to remember that the new identity will itself necessarily exclude certain groups of people, and that new conceptual systems will necessarily exclude certain ideas. Whatever we decide, our views will be less dogmatic and more sincere once they have been deconstructed.

Further Reading

Note: This section is not intended to provide an exhaustive bibliography, but point the reader towards those sources that are most useful.

General introductions

The best historical survey of philosophy is still Bertrand Russell's *History of Western Philosophy*, a masterpiece first published in 1946 and reprinted by Routledge (London, 1991). However, Russell tends to focus on the shortcomings of his predecessors. In the same mould is the less comprehensive but highly entertaining *The Story of Philosophy* by Will Durant (London: Ernest Benn, 1962). A more constructive approach is taken by Anthony Gottlieb's excellent study, *The Dream of Reason* (London: Allen Lane, 2000), which highlights the way in which ancient ideas informed their modern counterparts. A fine exponent of the philosophical treatise as instruction manual is the American philosopher Roy Sorensen – see, for example, *Pseudo-Problems* (London: Routledge, 1993). For a primer in the formal and technical aspects of logic and argumentation intended for students, *Critical Thinking* (Peterborough, Ont.: Broadview Press, 2000) by W. Hughes is among the clearest.

I Thales's Well

None of Thales's works – if indeed there were any – survive, but Aristotle wrote of the philosopher and his ideas in the *Metaphysics* and *Politics*. Other, less reliable, accounts come to us through Diogenes Laertius's *Lives of Eminent Philosophers*, trans. R. D. Hicks (London: William Heinemann, 1925) written in the sixth century AD and Herodotus's *Histories* from the fifth century BC. There are few definitive philosophical accounts of reductionist thinking, and the best sense of how it works is given by any good example of popular science from *A Brief History of Time* by Stephen W. Hawking (London: Bantam, 1988) to Steven Pinker's *How the Mind Works* (London: Norton, 1997). Cornell University's research on the chemical basis of love was reported in the *Sunday Times* (London), 1 August 1999.

2 Protagoras and the Pigs

Socrates' demolition of Protagoras is given in Plato's *Theaetetus* in *Plato: the Collected Dialogues*, ed. Edith Hamilton and Huntington Cairns (Princeton University Press, 1961). A sophisticated discussion of relativism is given by Bernard Williams in *Ethics and the Limits of Philosophy* (London: Fontana, 1985). Alasdair MacIntyre offers a historical approach to relativism in the excellent *After Virtue* (London: Duckworth, 1981). *The View From Nowhere* by Thomas Nagel (Oxford University Press, 1986) on the wider implications of subjectivity stands as a classic for both the academic and general reader. The misfortunes of Sting are recounted in *Wild in the Woods: the Myth of the Noble Eco-Savage* by Robert Whelan, pp. 48–50 (IEA Studies on the Environment, No. 14, published by the IEA Environment Unit, 1999).

3 Zeno and the Tortoise

Zeno's paradoxes of motion are examined in Aristotle's *Physics*, VI.9, VIII.8. They are considered alongside other issues in *The Infinite* by A. W. Moore (London: Routledge, 1990). Much of this book is intended for specialists, but its opening and final chapters can be understood and appreciated by all. *Paradoxes* (Cambridge University Press, 1988) by R. M. Sainsbury presents a comprehensive inventory of classic philosophical paradoxes.

4 The Socratic Inquisition

The two original sources for the words of Socrates are Plato's dialogues and Xenophon's *Apology*, *Symposium*, and *Memorabilia*. In *Socrates: Philosophy in Plato's Early Dialogues* (London: Routledge & Kegan Paul, 1979), Gerasimos Xenophon Santas attempts to draw the opinions of the philosopher out from those of his pupil. I. F. Stone's *The Trial of Socrates* (London: Jonathan Cape, 1988) gives the Athenian side of the story in the philosopher's execution.

5 Plato's Cave

The Platonic project and its later fortunes are examined at length in Iris Murdoch's *Metaphysics as a Guide to Morals* (London: Penguin, 1993). Hilary Putnam's suggestion that consciousness is software is reprinted in *Philosophical Papers*, vol. 2: *Mind, Language and Reality* (Cambridge University Press, 1975). William Paley, Archdeacon of Carlisle, presented his watchmaker analogy in *Natural Theology* (London: R. Faulder, 1802).

6 Aristotle's Goals

Aristotle's two works on morality are *The Nicomachean Ethics* and *The Eudemian Ethics*, while teleology is discussed more generally in the *Physics*. These texts can be found in *The Complete Works of Aristotle*, ed. Jonathan Barnes (Princeton University Press, 1984). *Ethics with Aristotle* by Sarah Broadie (Oxford University Press, 1991) is a good next step. For excellent examples of Darwinian thought, see *The Blind Watchmaker* (London: Penguin, 1986) and *The Selfish Gene* (Oxford University Press, 1976) by Richard Dawkins.

7 Lucretius's Spear

Lucretius's *On the Nature of Things* is published by Penguin (1974), translated by R. E. Latham. David Wiggins examines split-brain cases in *Sameness and Substance* (Oxford: Blackwell, 1980). The Ship of Theseus and other examples are examined by Harold Noonan in *Personal Identity* (London: Routledge, 1989), while a complex and moving account of the absence of personal identity is found in *Reasons and Persons* by Derek Parfit (Oxford: Clarendon Press, 1984). Roy Sorensen's *Thought Experiments* (Oxford University Press, 1992) provides an exhaustive but always entertaining study of the form.

8 Ockham's Razor

William of Ockham's essential thoughts are gathered in *Philosophical Writings* (Edinburgh: Nelson, 1957), ed. and trans. Philotheus Boehner, while *The Cambridge Companion to Ockham*, ed. Paul Vincent Spade (Cambridge University Press, 1999), contains a good selection of critical articles. A great deal of densely presented background material to Ockham's ideas and times can be found in F. C. Copleston's *A History of Medieval Philosophy* (London: Methuen, 1972).

9 Machiavelli's Prince

Machiavelli's two main works are *The Prince* (London: Everyman, 1992) and *Discourses* (London: Penguin, 1983). Operation Restore Hope is chronicled by the war correspondent Scott Petersen in the instructive *Me Against My Brother* (New York: Routledge, 2000). George Stephanopoulos records Bill Clinton's colourful language in *All Too Human* (London: Hutchinson, 1999). *The New Machiavelli: the Art of Politics in Business* (Chichester: John Wiley, 1998) by Alistair McAlpine applies Machiavelli's ideas to the relationships between business leaders and their employees and shareholders. This book was greatly enjoyed by Margaret Thatcher.

10 Bacon's Chickens

Francis Bacon's *Novum Organum* is published by Open Court Publishing (Chicago, 1994), ed. Peter Urbach, though his *Essays* (Harmondsworth: Penguin, 1985) are far more accessible to the general reader. Bertrand Russell introduces his chickens in *The Problems of Philosophy* (Home University Library of Modern Knowledge, 1912), while Peter Strawson argues for the rationality of inductive thinking in *Introduction to Logical Theory* (London: Methuen, 1952).

11 Descartes' Demon

Bernard Williams gives a difficult but highly regarded account of Cartesian doubt in *Descartes: the Project of Pure Enquiry* (Hassocks: Harvester Press, 1978). Much simpler, but still giving a coherent account of Descartes' system of thought, is *Descartes* (London: Allen Lane, 1974) by Jonathan Rée. Ludwig Wittgenstein outlines the logical limits of our capacity to doubt in *On Certainty*, trans. Denis Paul and G. E. M. Anscombe (Oxford: Basil Blackwell, 1969). Demons and dreamers have been replaced by brains in vats as the thought experiment of choice in the study of scepticism and doubt – the subject of the dazzling first chapter of *Reason, Truth and History* by Hilary Putnam (Cambridge University Press, 1981).

12 Hume's Fork

The lucidity of Hume's writing means that all his works can be recommended, even for introductory readers. The two primary texts are *Enquiry Concerning Human Understanding* (Chicago: Open Court Publishing, 1988) and *A Treatise of Human Nature* (Oxford: Clarendon University Press, 1978).

13 Reid's Common Sense

Thomas Reid's *An Inquiry into the Human Mind on the Principles of Common Sense* is published by Edinburgh University Press (1997). His ideas were revived by G. E. Moore in 'A Defence of Common Sense', *Philosophical Papers* (London: George Allen & Unwin, 1959).

14 Rousseau's Contract

A new edition of *The Social Contract* was published in 1996 by Everyman. For two diametrically opposed accounts of the philosopher's life and work, read first Rousseau's *Confessions* (Oxford University Press, 2000), then the historian Paul Johnson's compelling, if extremely one-sided, demolition of Rousseau's work and character in *Intellectuals* (London: Weidenfeld & Nicolson, 1988).

15 Kant's Spectacles

The most faithful translation of Kant's *Critique of Pure Reason* is by Norman Kemp Smith (London: Macmillan, 1923). To the introductory reader it will only be episodically meaningful, however, so several general introductions to the philosopher are recommended prior to tackling his masterpiece. The best short guide to Kant's ideas is *Kant* by Roger Scruton (Oxford University Press, 1992), though Stephan Körner's *Kant* (Harmondsworth: Penguin, 1955) is also good.

16 Bentham's Calculus

The two canonical expositions of utilitarian thought are Bentham's own in *The Principles of Morals and Legislation* (Amherst, NY: Prometheus Books, 1988) and that of his successor John Stuart Mill in *Utilitarianism* (Oxford University Press, 1998). *Utilitarianism: For and Against* by J. J. C. Smart and Bernard Williams (Cambridge University Press, 1973) gives many vivid examples of the moral calculus in practice.

17 Hegel's Dialectic

Hegel's work is almost unreadable to all but specialists (and even to some specialists), as can be seen from *The Phenomenology of Spirit*, trans. A. V. Miller (Oxford University Press, 1979). Charles Taylor's *Hegel* (Cambridge University Press, 1975) is an extremely rigorous exposition, but not one recommended for beginners. More introductory is *Hegel on History* by Joseph McCarney (London: Routledge, 2000). A commendably clear and straightforward study is Robert Stern's *Hegel's Phenomenology of Spirit and Logic* (London: Routledge, 1993). A classic in its own right is Herbert Marcuse's *Reason and Revolution* (Oxford University Press, 1941), a meditation on Hegel's origins and influence up to the Second World War.

18 Nietzsche's Hammer

Virtually everything that Nietzsche wrote makes exhilarating reading. His central texts are *Beyond Good and Evil* and *On the Genealogy of Morals*, translated best by Walter Kaufmann in *Basic Writings of Nietzsche* (New York: Modern Library, 1992). His thoughts are given lyrical form in *Thus Spoke Zarathustra* (New York: Modern Library, 1995), also translated by Kaufmann – whose version of *Twilight of the Idols* can be found in *The Portable Nietzsche* (London: Chatto & Windus, 1971). *Nietzsche as*

Philosopher (London: Collier-Macmillan, 1965) by Arthur C. Danto is a helpful aid to understanding Nietzsche. Alexander Nehamas writes on the philosopher with some verve in *Nietzsche: Life as Literature* (Harvard University Press, 1985).

19 The Young Wittgenstein's Mirror

Wittgenstein's *Tractatus Logico-Philosophicus* (London: Routledge & Kegan Paul, 1961), trans. D. F. Pears and Brian McGuinness, is the main source of his early philosophy. Ray Monk's seminal biography, *Ludwig Wittgenstein: the Duty of Genius* (London: Jonathan Cape, 1990), is both an absorbing study of the philosopher's life and a good introduction to his ideas. Allan Janik and Stephen Toulmin present a vivid rendering of the philosopher's birthplace and its contribution to his thought in *Wittgenstein's Vienna* (London: Weidenfeld & Nicolson, 1973). The letter to von Ficker is reprinted in 'Letters to Ludwig von Ficker', ed. A. Janik, trans. B. Gillette in *Wittgenstein: Sources and Perspectives*, ed. C. G. Luckhardt (Harvester, 1979).

20 The Older Wittgenstein's Games

The chief source of Wittgenstein's later thought is *Philosophical Investigations*, trans. G. E. M. Anscombe (Oxford: Basil Blackwell, 1953). Ernest Gellner conducted a brilliant attack on Wittgenstein's work and influence in *Words and Things* (London: Victor Gollancz, 1959). For those who distrust the 'logic-chopping' of Anglo-American philosophers, this book is the antidote. However, Marie McGinn perhaps presents a clearer understanding of Wittgenstein and his work in *Wittgenstein and the Philosophical Investigations* (London: Routledge, 1997).

21 Popper's Dolls

Popper's two great works are *The Logic of Scientific Discovery* (London: Hutchinson, 1959) and *The Open Society and its Enemies* (London: Routledge & Sons, 1945). Bryan Magee's *Philosophy and the Real World: An Introduction to Karl Popper* (London: Fontana, 1973) is difficult to get hold of, but Magee also writes engagingly on Popper in *Confessions of a Philosopher* (London: Weidenfeld & Nicolson, 1997).

22 Ryle's University

Ryle propounded his ideas in *The Concept of Mind* (London: Hutchinson's University Library, 1949). *Ryle*, ed. Oscar P. Wood and George Pitcher (London: Macmillan, 1971) contains a brief autobiography by the philosopher and a collection of essays on his work by writers such as A. J. Ayer and J. L. Austin. Douglas R. Hofstadter takes an imaginative look at emergence in *Goedel, Escher, Bach* (Hassocks: Harvester Press, 1979).

23 Turing's Machine
Searle first proposed his Chinese room experiment in 'Minds, Brains, and Programs', *Behavioral and Brain Sciences* 3 (Cambridge University Press, 1980). Objections to Searle's arguments are expertly advanced by Daniel C. Dennett in *Consciousness Explained* (London: Allen Lane, 1992), a book which also gives something of a masterclass in the use of philosophical tools and techniques. *The Mind's I*, ed. Douglas R. Hofstadter and Daniel C. Dennett (Brighton: Harvester Press, 1981) is an anthology containing several excellent articles on consciousness and machine intelligence.

24 Dawkins's Meme
The Selfish Gene by Richard Dawkins was first published in 1976 by Oxford University Press. The best account of memetics to date has been Susan Blackmore's *The Meme Machine* (Oxford University Press, 1999). There is also an excellent chapter in Daniel C. Dennett's *Darwin's Dangerous Idea* (London: Allen Lane, 1995) on the prospects of a science of memes.

25 Derrida and Deconstruction
None of Derrida's texts can be recommended for the beginner. *Writing and Difference*, trans. Alan Bass (London: Routledge & Kegan Paul, 1978) is supposedly introductory but will be unintelligible even to most readers with a grounding in philosophy. Slightly easier to comprehend is *Limited Inc.*, trans. Samuel Weber and Jeffrey Mehlman (Evanston, IL: Northwestern University Press, 1988), in which Derrida is forced to make sense in order to answer the philosopher John Searle's criticisms. Derrida discusses Plato's *Phaedrus* in detail in *Dissemination*, trans. Barbara Johnson (London: Athlone Press, 1981). The Izutsu letter and the interview with *Le Nouvel Observateur* are reprinted in *Derrida & Différance*, eds. David Wood and Robert Bernasconi (Coventry: Parousia Press, 1985). The writings of Christopher Norris are of great help in deciphering Derrida's texts: see *Derrida* (London: Fontana, 1987) and *Deconstruction and the Unfinished Project of Modernity* (London: Athlone Press, 2000).

Index

Absolute Spirit 119
Academy, the 34–5, 42–3
Achilles 20–22
Adler, Alfred 145
aesthetics 118, 135
Alcibiades 26
Alexander the Great 42–3
altruism 166
American Revolution 100
  Declaration of
    Independence 100
analogies 31–40, 132, 172
  of the cave 36–8
  of the soul with the eye
    37–8
  of the watch 33
animal rights 39–40
antithesis 119–20, 173
Aristotle 3–4, 41–9, 73–4
  On the Generation of Animals
    46
  On Kingship 42
atheism 170
Athens 20, 30, 42–3
Austin, J. L. 151

Bacon, Sir Francis 47, 68–70,
  72
beauty 107

Becher, Johann 154
behaviourists 58–9
Bentham, Jeremy 109–12, 115
Berkeley, George 92
Black, Joseph 154
Blake, William 2
Borgia, Cesare 63
Brahms, Johannes 130

Callisthenes of Olynthus 43
Camus, Albert 174
'category mistake' 152–3
cause and effect 85, 89, 106,
  154
character 81, 87
Charlemont, Earl of 83
Christianity 45, 125–6, 129
Cogito ergo sum 77–8
common sense 85, 88–95
computers 161–4
consciousness 151, 153–5, 162
Copernicus 74, 165
Crick, Francis 165
cultural tolerance 16–17

Darwin, Charles 33, 46, 70
  The Origin of Species 45, 165
Dawkins, Richard 165–70
  The Blind Watchmaker 33

The Selfish Gene 165–6
deconstruction 173, 175–80
Delacroix, Eugène 98
Delphi 3, 27
democracy 101
Democritus 43
Derrida, Jacques 173–80
   Dissemination 176
Descartes, René 73–8, 151, 154
dialectic 116, 119–21
Diderot, Denis 98
doppelgänger 53
doubt 73, 75–80

Einstein, Albert 146
emergence 153–4, 156–7
empiricism 92, 104–6
Encyclopédie 98
Enlightenment, the 74, 97, 118
'epiphenomenal' states 155,
   157
essences 57
ethics 40–41, 90, 135, 138–9
eudaimonia 48–9

falsification 147–9
Feynman, Richard 2
Ficker, Ludwig von 135
'final ends' 43–8
Florence 61–2
Fodor, Jerry 6
'form of life' 141, 143
Forms, theory of 35
free will 154, 156–7
freedom 116, 119–20
French Revolution 100

Freud, Sigmund 2, 145–6,
   148

Galileo 37, 62, 74
genes 165–9, 171–2
geometry 75, 82, 84
Germany 117
God 33, 45, 56–7, 59, 62, 76–8,
   96, 105–6, 111, 125, 129, 136
'Good', the 38–9
Gorgias 11, 25
grammar 151, 153

Hamilton, William 166
happiness 110–11, 115
'hedonic calculus' 111–15
Hegel, Georg 116–21
   The Phenomenology of Spirit
   117
Herodotus 3
history 122, 125
Hobbes, Thomas 99
human rights 16, 115
humanism 62
Hume, David 71, 81–7, 89–90,
   92, 104–5
   A Treatise of Human Nature
   82
Hume's Fork 85, 103
hypothetical scenarios 50–55

idealism 92
identity 52–4
induction 67–72, 147
instincts 89, 91, 93–5
Izutsu, Professor 175

Kant, Immanuel 23, 103–8,
    112, 125, 130
    Religion Within the
        Boundaries of Pure Reason
        104
Keynes, John Maynard 138
knowledge 105–8

language 130, 132–8, 140,
    142–4, 162–4, 176, 180
    games 138–44
law 110, 112, 120
Le Vasseur, Thérèse 98, 101
Leibniz, Gottfried 150
    Monadology 150
Locke, John 92–3, 103
logic 23, 32, 71, 125, 160
Lombard, Peter 56
Lucretius, Titus Carus 50
Lyceum, the 43

Machiavelli, Niccolò 61–6
    The Prince 61–3
McCosh, James 88
machines 161–4
    Colossus 160–61
    Enigma 160
    Turing 164
    'universal' 160
MacIntyre, Alasdair 81
Magee, Bryan 146
Marx, Karl 2, 121, 145–6
materialism 99, 121, 151,
    156–7
mathematics 75, 82, 84–7, 131,
    159, 162

Medici, Lorenzo de' 61
memes 168–72
Mendel, Gregor 46
mental states 59, 92, 156
metaphors 177
metaphysics 105–6, 151
Miletus 2, 4
Mill, James 111
Mill, John Stuart 111, 156
mind 151–5, 157, 161–2, 164
Montaigne, Michel de 73
Moore, G. E. 93
morality 15–18, 23, 39–40, 90,
    107, 109, 111–15, 125–6, 130
Morcom, Christopher 159

Napoleon 110, 117
nation-state 120
nationalism 117, 124
Natural Law 96
natural selection 33, 45–6,
    166
nature 33, 39–40, 68–9, 71
    laws of 67, 70, 85, 89
    state of 120
Nazism 16, 101, 124
necessity 85–6
Nietzsche, Friedrich 89–90,
    122–9
    The Antichrist 123
    Ecce Homo 124
    Thus Spake Zarathustra 123
    Twilight of the Idols 122–3
'noble savages' 99
nominalism 58
'noumena' 106

Ockham, William of 56–8, 60, 93–4
Ockham's Razor 56–60, 107
ontological argument 77

Paley, William 33
'Panopticon' 110–11
paradoxes 20–22
  of Achilles and the tortoise 20–22
  of the arrow 21–2
  of the racetrack 21–2
Parmenides 19–20
Pater, Walter 2
perceptions 12–13, 38, 92–3, 102, 105, 107, 130
Plato 3, 11, 19–20, 28, 34–9, 42, 57, 105–6, 125, 142, 177
  dialogues 34–5
  Phaedrus 176
  The Republic 36
  Theaetetus 12
Platonism 126
politics 61–6
Popper, Sir Karl 145–7
  The Open Society 146
'private language argument' 140
Protagoras 10–15, 18, 25
Putnam, Hilary 32

quantum theory 91, 146, 156

racism 124
Ramsey, Frank 134
rationalism 104

realism 61
reason 48, 87, 91, 104–5, 118, 144
reductio ad absurdum 19, 22–4
reductionism 1–2, 4–9, 151–2, 155–7
Reid, James Gregory 88
Reid, Thomas 88–95
relativism 10, 12–15
relativity 146
religion 169–71
replicability 167
Ritschl, Friedrich Wilhelm 123
Rousseau, Jean-Jacques 83, 97–101
  Émile 104
  The Social Contract 99
rules 138–42, 144, 159–62, 164
Russell, Bertrand 46, 67–8, 72, 88, 120, 131
Ryle, Gilbert 150–53, 155
  The Concept of Mind 151

St Augustine of Hippo 56
Saussure, Ferdinand de 177
scepticism 89–93, 103
Schopenhauer, Arthur 118
Schrödinger, Erwin 91
Searle, John 163–4
self 53–4, 85
Seven Sages 3
Ship of Theseus 52–3
signs 135, 177, 179
Smith, John Maynard 166
social contract 97, 99–101

Socrates 11, 12, 20, 25–30, 34–5, 37, 43
Socratic method 25–9
sophists 11, 25–7
Speusippus 42–3
Stalinism 101
Stoicism 128
suffering 127–9
synthesis 119–20

tabula rasa 103
Tallis, Raymond 175
teleology 41, 46–7
telos 44
Thales 2–5
thesis 119–20
thought experiments 50–55, 113
Thrace 10
'transcendental criticism' 104
Travers, Robert 166
truth 11, 15, 25–7, 29, 35–6, 38–9, 42, 107–8, 116, 119, 124–5, 127, 130, 133, 136–9, 141, 143

Turing, Alan 159–62
Turing test 161–2, 164

Übermensch 122, 124, 129
utilitarianism 109–15
utopia 100

Wagner, Richard 123–4
Warens, Madame de 98
Watson, James 165
Wiggins, David 53–4
'Will to Power' 122, 125–7
Williams, Bernard 113
Williams, George 166
Wittgenstein, Ludwig 58, 130–32, 134–44, 162
    Philosophical Investigations 142, 178
    Tractatus Logico-Philosophicus 131, 134–5, 142
writing 176–7

Xenocrates 42–3

Zeno 19–22